# ARRIVAL PRESS

## POETS AROUND BRITAIN

Edited

By

SUZY GOODALL

First published in Great Britain in 1995 by
ARRIVAL PRESS
1 - 2 Wainman Road, Woodston,
Peterborough, PE2 7BU

All Rights Reserved

**Copyright Contributors 1995**


SB ISBN 1 85786 356 9

# *FOREWORD*

'Poets around Britain' is a collection of verse that gives an insight into how local writers feel about the areas in which they live. Among poems about the landscape and nature, nestle works about individuals, the community and their way of life.

I am sure that you will enjoy reading 'Poets Around Britain', and savour this poetic tour guide in the comfort of your own armchair.


Suzy Goodall
Editor

# CONTENTS

| | | |
|---|---|---|
| Littlehampton - Good Morning | Doris E Hymas | 1 |
| A Forest And Strange Sheep Remembered | J H Absalom | 2 |
| Littledean Hill Road | Kathleen J Smith | 3 |
| Twilight On The Malverns | Stewart Richards | 4 |
| Worthing | Ashley Montanaro | 4 |
| Symonds Yat | Joyce Latham | 5 |
| Thanet In Kent | W Collett | 6 |
| Untitled | Norma Collins | 6 |
| Dear Tonbridge, Yours Faithfully | Ralph Stott | 7 |
| Christmas In Pevensey | Judith Moore | 8 |
| Stonehenge | Judy Gaskell | 8 |
| Eastbourne | Tim Caroe | 9 |
| The Cross | Catherine Jones | 9 |
| The Village Pond | Doug Thomas | 10 |
| Past And Present | Carol O'Connor | 11 |
| Lights On Oldham Edge | Scott Richardson | 11 |
| Mystery Tour | Hilda Brown | 12 |
| Medway Towns - So Part Of Kent | C Saunders | 13 |
| Eastbourne, UK | J Power | 14 |
| Old Reading Town | June Marshall | 14 |
| Round Cranbrook Town | H M Funnell | 15 |
| Southwick Green | David Jackson | 16 |
| A Town For All Seasons | Elsie Anderson | 17 |
| Sissinghurst Castle, Kent | Henry J Green | 18 |
| The Fishers Of Ross | Jean Semple | 19 |
| The Captive | Anna Marion-Cox | 20 |
| The Unchanging Scene | Roy Smith | 21 |
| Brading Down | C West | 22 |
| Untitled | Ron Delacruz | 22 |
| Weymouth Beach | Shirley M Foster | 23 |
| Chapel Close | Raymond White | 24 |
| Retirement-Ville | Mae Smith | 25 |
| Clogging Up Medway! | Wendy A Cudd | 26 |

| | | |
|---|---|---|
| Basingstoke Alive! | Margaret E Gaines | 27 |
| Swindon | Steve Clarke | 28 |
| Where Else But In England | A McFarline | 29 |
| Friendly Wimborne | Ann Chambers | 30 |
| River Stour | Aileen Hawkins | 30 |
| Dorset Cameos | John Paget | 31 |
| Dancing Ledge | Stephanie McGurk | 32 |
| Merley | Leslie H Brown | 33 |
| My Town | R Walch | 33 |
| Foster's School, Sherborne | John Paulley | 34 |
| Tyneham Village | Townley Shenton | 35 |
| Untitled | Heather Wannell | 35 |
| Kent | W Todd | 36 |
| Village Fete (Appleshaw) | Gwynneth Curtis | 37 |
| Three Local Views | Frank Pickering | 38 |
| Dorset Newcomers | Sheila Beattie | 39 |
| Chesil Beach | Sue White | 40 |
| Place Names | Alan Potter | 40 |
| Modern Dorset Poet Answers Back | V H Anderson | 41 |
| New Forest Nightmare | Doug Gregory | 42 |
| From Here You Can Smell The Brewery | Rosemary Price | 43 |
| A Day Out In Blackpool | Margaret Wilson | 44 |
| Lakeland Pride | Susan Bell | 45 |
| On Rivington Pike | Eric Holt | 46 |
| Baiter Point | Dorothy Davis-Sellick | 47 |
| Woodseaves, Herefordshire | William Austin Pugh | 48 |
| A Liverpool Triolet | Barbara Gillett | 49 |
| The Halcyon South | Heather Rayner | 50 |
| The Isle Of Three Legs | Eve Clucas | 51 |
| A Lancashire Party | Elizabeth Powell | 52 |
| Wet North West! | Jenny Golds | 53 |
| Muncaster Castle | Barbara Kemp | 54 |
| Lancashire - Not As Black As | Sue Gerrard | 54 |
| Lancashire | Jim Bland | 55 |
| Cheshire Is Home | Helen Johnson | 56 |
| Lancashire Life | Eileen Lloyd | 57 |

| | | |
|---|---|---|
| Broadstone | Patricia Thomas | 58 |
| Dorset Landscape | Christine Llewellyn | 59 |
| Northern Exposure | S Armah | 60 |
| Kernow (Cornwall) | Sandra Austin | 60 |
| King Cotton | Edith Freeman | 61 |
| The Railway Umbrella | E M Fogel | 62 |
| Ulverston - The Town | N Ronson | 63 |
| Aspects Of The Inner City | Heather Render | 64 |
| My Island | Lorna Viol | 64 |
| Ormsgill Reservoir | Ayelet McKenzie | 65 |
| England Forever . . . | Ann Lander | 66 |
| Wigan Carnival | Dorothy McDonald | 67 |
| Wigan Market | Thomas Arthur Pendlebury | 68 |
| Poulton-Le-Fylde | Frank Turner | 69 |
| At Last | Cecil R Bradbury | 69 |
| The Saul Street Baths | Christine Meredith | 70 |
| This Wiltshire Life | I Sainsbury | 70 |
| Untitled | C V Nally | 71 |
| A Day In The Lakeland | Máire Cowley | 72 |
| Dent Foot Chapel | Daisy Cooper | 73 |
| A Saturday Night At Home 1949 | Peter O'Keeffe | 74 |
| Castleshaw Roman Fort, Saddleworth | Peter J Wren | 75 |
| Dee Estuary In April | John Clifford | 76 |
| The New Spire On Stowmarket Church | Elizabeth Cook | 77 |
| Waterloo Keg Day | G Marshall | 78 |
| In My Sussex Garden | Stephen Gunner | 78 |
| Mardale | Marion Jones | 79 |
| Aquae Sulis | Marie Bowerman-Taylor | 80 |
| The Flower Stall At Beccles | A M Bowles | 81 |
| The Lane In Town | K Scarfe | 82 |
| Nearby To Loughton | Carol Ross | 83 |
| Essex | Peter Hewing | 84 |
| A Little Bit Of Norfolk | Anthony Paul | 84 |
| Thetford | Daphne Flello | 85 |
| The Village Church | B Salter | 86 |

| | | |
|---|---|---|
| Changing Dartford | Irene Seager | 87 |
| On The Downs Above Southwick | Chris Goodwin | 88 |
| Plumpton Plain Dig | E Westbury | 88 |
| West Sussex | Elizabeth Rodgers | 89 |
| A Centurion On Selsey | Brenda Choppen | 90 |
| A Town Of Renown | Frances Green | 91 |
| The South | Marina Roberts | 92 |
| Kent - Gateway To Europe | Diana Cole | 92 |
| My County | Anji Tuppen | 93 |
| Sussex | Neville Croll | 94 |
| A Windy Day In Croft Woods | June Newton | 95 |
| Dark Side | Kathleen Clarke | 95 |
| All Saints, Shropshire | Bill Woods | 96 |
| Egdon Heath | A Crabb | 97 |
| A Place To Visit | Barbara Froggatt | 98 |
| Grinsel Hill | E Balmain | 98 |
| Croft Ambrey | M Checketts | 99 |
| Warrington Bombings | David Geldard | 100 |
| The Church Of Logs | Kathleen Barker | 100 |
| Lost And Found | Anne Torrington | 101 |
| Cerne Giant | M D Pike | 102 |
| Oswalds (Near Lulworth Cove) | Devina Symes | 102 |
| A Special Place | Roy Hawker | 103 |
| Shingle Street Mystery | June Trelawny | 104 |
| Essex Life | B M Mynard | 105 |
| Norfolk County | Kaz Holman | 106 |
| Where Sheep Safely Graze | Violet Croad | 106 |
| North Norfolk | B I Dawson | 107 |
| Durham Miners Gala | Gil Vincent | 108 |
| Essex | T A Tuvey | 109 |
| Felixstowe | B Smith | 110 |
| The River Avon - Winding Its Way From Bath | C Cottingham | 111 |
| Avon Aurora | Julia Hemings | 112 |
| Evening On Watchet Beach | Barbara Hine | 112 |
| Gloucester City | Heidi Bevan | 113 |

| | | |
|---|---|---|
| Weobley | Tim Barnes | 114 |
| Civitas In Bello Et Pace Fidelis | David Ind | 115 |
| Avon, My Haven | Rose Anderton | 116 |
| Dean Home | Heather Geddes | 116 |
| To The Visitor Of Herefordshire | Stan Pinches | 117 |
| The Legend Of Esselie (Ashley) Church | M Haslehurst | 118 |
| Thank Your Lucky Stars | Gill Ricketts | 119 |
| The River Severn | J Selwyn | 119 |
| The Malvern Way | Heather Perrott | 120 |
| Cold Feet | David Clement | 121 |
| The Severn Bore | Joe Silver | 121 |
| Hills Of Home | Betty Mealand | 122 |
| Down By The Miry Brook | Bill Reid | 123 |
| Gentle Ladies | Meg Pybus | 124 |
| Peace | E Ozanne | 124 |
| To The Hills Of Home | Beryl V Pardoe | 125 |
| The New Gloucester City | Shirley M Watson | 126 |
| New Town By Night | J Mutchell | 127 |
| Pharaoh's Lighthouse, Fleetwood | Dot Walmsley | 128 |
| Rising Severn | Ivy Lee | 128 |
| Hereford Station | Terence Hutchins | 129 |
| Swineside Valley | Barbara Eastham | 130 |
| On Central Pier | John Tirebuck | 131 |
| Somerset, Somerset | Nicholas Winn | 132 |
| The Haunted Church | A Dolan | 133 |
| View From Pilling Shore (Part 2) | Mack A Duerden | 134 |
| My Lancashire | Esma Banham | 135 |
| Oh Lancashire | David Charnley | 136 |
| Glevum | Jean Price | 136 |
| Looking Towards Gloucester From Longford | Eleanor West | 137 |
| Behind The Candy Floss | Beryl Kearns | 138 |
| The Dell At Hunt End | Jamie Lewis | 139 |

| | | |
|---|---|---|
| Season Curls | Valerie J Knopp | 139 |
| Weston Super Mare | M E Beale | 140 |
| Avalon | Bob Woodroofe | 142 |
| Gloucestershire Churches | Diana Maslen | 143 |
| Bronze Age Boat | Edwina Gray | 144 |
| The View From My Window | Anne Dearle | 145 |
| On Route A29 | A Richards | 146 |
| Cuckmere | P Byers | 147 |
| Avon Radio Report | Judith Corrigan | 148 |
| Come And See | Jacqui Pittock | 149 |
| Kent's River | Michael J Hills | 150 |
| Sounds Of Harmony | Mary West | 150 |
| Old Mother Goring | Joyce Birchall | 151 |
| From Home . . . By Train | Moreen Smythe | 152 |
| South Eastern England | S Knowles | 153 |
| Kent | V Weston | 154 |
| Dear Dover | Winnie May | 154 |
| Our Park | Monica F Leppard | 155 |
| From A Stile In Kent (1981) | M J Timms | 156 |
| The Joy Of The Garden Of England | Geoffrey J Martin | 157 |
| Here In Kent | Sheralyn Kent | 158 |
| Bexleyheath Broadway | Maggie Sparvell | 159 |
| Margate | Kate Beerling | 160 |
| The Counties Of Kent And East Sussex | Isabella M Collier | 161 |
| Place Names | Mercia MacDermott | 162 |
| Chichester Yacht Basin - A Fantasy | Flora Groves | 163 |
| You Know You're In Yorkshire When . . . | Irene Taylor | 164 |
| Canterbury | Roy R Hackers | 164 |
| Nostalgic Wistfulness | J Bryant | 165 |
| Seven Sisters | Aubrey M Woolman | 166 |
| Kent | B Hussey | 167 |
| Legananny | William Dunlop | 167 |
| Southern Views | David Jenkins | 168 |
| Contrasting Essex | J Little | 168 |

| | | |
|---|---|---|
| Beachy Head | M E Lang | 169 |
| Christmas Presents - | | |
|   Trying Out Bikes | Patrick Taylor | 170 |
| Curran Road (Lively Folk!) | Rita O'Rourke | 171 |
| Down Towns Antiques | Carson Scott | 172 |
| The Old Swinging Bridge | Tom McTaggart | 173 |
| A Dorset Roman Road | Mary S Evans | 174 |
| Beneath The Southern Sun | June Rampton | 175 |
| Beer: A Devon Village | Nicky Dicken-Fuller | 176 |
| Poole | E Sharpley | 177 |
| My El Dorado | Ena Wilson | 178 |
| The Immigrant's Dream | Betty Hueston | 179 |
| Deadman's Lane | David Brasier | 179 |
| Ambassadors In Red And Blue | Norm Whittle | 180 |
| Bramford | Sue Rhodes | 181 |
| Irstead Staithe | Margaret Vernon | 182 |
| Roman Camulodunum | Brian A Cooke | 182 |
| The Hospice At Colchester | Ken Moore | 183 |
| My Street | Linda Roberts | 184 |
| Why Essex? | Sonia J Lister | 185 |
| Norwich City | D M Stone | 186 |
| The Message Of The Bells | Maureen Crampin | 187 |
| The Knights Of Essex '95 | Barbara Fosh | 188 |
| Norwich And Its Niche | | |
|   In The Universe | Dale Craske | 189 |
| Marsh Mill | Malcolm F Andrews | 190 |
| Kent | Lynda M Bourne | 190 |
| The Winds Of Time | D Cain | 191 |
| Silence At The Mill | David A Garside | 192 |

## LITTLEHAMPTON - GOOD MORNING

No storm today; no wind; praise be;
A sparkling blue, sun-dappled sea,
Where speed boats scud across the waves,
And, from the far horizon haze
A freighter takes amorphous shape
To start its long and patient wait
For harbourage.
The pilot boat will bring her in.
With very careful shepherding,
To tie up in the Arun, while
The river shows a carefree style,
With all the ocean-going boats
That sail away for hours afloat -
Quite different from the winter, when
We wave to hardy fishermen.

The children now have found the sands,
Spades and buckets in tiny hands;
Perhaps they'll ride the Noddy train,
Along the *prom* and back again:
Or will the fine amusement park
Provide the final magic spark?
The day is theirs; unbounded joy
For every little girl and boy,
And for us, too, the memory stays
Through all of time to any age,
Of just how wonderful can be
A summer morning by the sea.

*Doris E Hymas*

## A FOREST AND STRANGE SHEEP REMEMBERED

To the west of the Severn I travel
To a separate world. For peace.
Where the Queen's verderer wields the gavel
In a courtroom in the Speech House among trees.

Say! Have you seen those odd sheep?

Small towns, small shops and hardy warm-hearted people.
Not unlike my own in the north.
Old churches with towers and an occasional strange steeple.
Bluebells, ferns, 'snompers' the breezes wave back and forth.

Ho! Keep your eye on those sheep!

They'll jump the vicar's gate at Parkend and
Leap a ten foot stone wall - I s'in 'em!
When you're driving quite fast you'll think of your past and
Cuss as they wander in flock. Single or tandem!

Thic sheep own the roads so watch 'em!

God save St Briavels and Clearwell with castle.
Yorkley, Cannop, Drybrook and Sling
Wander forest glades without hassle.
Meet poets and Morris dancers. Hear foresters sing.

But. Hey! - old butt' keep your gate shut to those sheep!

There, between Wales and England, in the Marches
Lies that separate place of renown.
Dean Forest with its oaks, lime, pine and larches
And Freeminers near Soudley, Coleford and Cinderford town.

Lords of this royal domain are those sheep!

Oh! Help me escape to the forest again.
Let me there once more own a plot
Where peace and quiet did always reign
And the rest of the world I forgot.

Like those wandering, strange sheep. I'd be free. Join me?

*J H Absalom*


## LITTLEDEAN HILL ROAD

There's a freshness in the air and each breath is pure and clean.
We push forward in the wind and it meets us with a keen
And glancing blow, but we toss its force aside,
And push onward to the topmost road,
The road now clear and wide.
There we pause awhile to view
A panoramic sight.
The fields are spread beneath us in a blanket green and bright.
They sweep down in giant curving lines below,
Where nestled snug and still,
The village lies, compact and small beneath this towering hill.
Each building detailed small but clear
As in a water-colour hung
Before our eyes, the school, the gaol,
The church - where even now the bells are rung.
Beyond the trees our eyes will idly stray
To where the Severn winds its weary way
To Gloucester and its busy docks, while here we stay
Above the noise of endless roads of traffic rushing to and fro.
Stand in the wind with face aglow
And view the cliffs at Severn's edge all red.

*Kathleen J Smith*

## TWILIGHT ON THE MALVERNS

The stream is singing down the mountain,
Pure water whispers on the hill.
My mind relaxes with the music,
As all else is still.

The moon is shining in the heavens,
Her silver light falls on the path.
Unreal perceptions cling to memory,
And I clutch my staff.

A crow is soaring on the thermals.
Black is his shadow on the sky.
Deep are my thoughts in lonely vigil
As he journeys by.

The wind is speaking in the tree tops.
Long have I loved him all my life.
To child and man the voice of calmness
In gladness or strife.

The ear and eye are thus awakened.
The mind is soothed by dusk's remorse.
The eerie time is for remembering
Our impending course.

*Stewart Richards*


## WORTHING

Beautiful sunsets all seen from our door
Trapped in the air over no town but ours.
No other town could have sunsets their twin
None could compare to the sunsets I've seen.
The sea here is ours; no other lays claim
Nowhere could waves be like these, just the same.
You can't wrap it up in bright, beautiful clothing;
It is still, however, so perfectly Worthing.

*Ashley Montanaro*

**SYMONDS YAT**

The wooded hills of Symonds Yat fall steeply to the Wye
And through their midst grey towering cliffs thrust upward to the sky.
On sunny days the traveller views a panoramic scene
From that majestic, well trod rock - fair jewel of our Dean.
Before our gaze a silver thread of glistening waters wend
In undulating twists and curves around a horseshoe bend.

But there's another, secret side, to Symonds' smiling face
Found lurking down its shady slopes - a strange, mysterious place
Where monster stones crouch silently beneath the oaks so tall
If they could speak I wonder what their memory would recall?

Long vanished seas, dark fathoms deep, where fish of every hue
Swam lazily through seaweed fronds which round about them grew.
Long years of cold, encased in ice, when mammoths roamed the earth,
And they have heard the lion roar, and watched the bear give birth.

Within their shade hyenas laughed, and woolly rhinos slept,
As in and out of secret caves primeval humans crept.
The Romans and Silurians in deadly combat met
Around these stones, their ancient bones perchance are resting yet.

Now snowdrops tumble down the banks when springtime comes around
And in their wake wild daffodils and bluebells can be found.
A timid deer flits silently between the light and shade
And pheasants screech when wily fox prowls softly through the glade.

A treasure trove of sights and sounds from Dean's long history
Lie locked inside these age old rocks, if we could find the key.

This world of ours holds many things for Man to wonder at,
But none I'll swear that can compare with lovely Symonds Yat.

*Joyce Latham*

## THANET IN KENT

There's no place to live like Thanet
As seasons change it's like another planet
In winter the trees are empty, wind so cold
But still it all feels so bold

And when the cold winds slip on by
People don't ask themselves why
They come to stay in Thanet in Kent
As the warm breeze drifts in, heaven sent

The miles of coast line of sea and sand
Thousands who visit here understand
It's a place filled with oh so much
Excitement tranquillity at a touch

Whatever your needs are likely to be
I'm sure this part of Kent will hold a key
To unlock your imagination and your heart
Which will make you never want to part

*W Collett*


## UNTITLED

Life in Gloucestershire is tranquil and serene
A slower pace than city ways
Where country paths meander
Babbling brooks and streams.
Arched bridges span the windrush, trout swim the river Coln.
Market squares still used, where once the wool was sold.
Roman and Saxon fortresses, roads which were made to last,
Mellow cottages of Cotswold stone - first built in times now past.

The smithy in his forge, the anvil throwing sparks,
A man who builds the hedgerows, to accommodate the larks
Miles of drystone walling, around the country lanes
Keeping in sheep and cattle, making sure they do not stray.

Patchwork land aglow with yellow rape and corn,
Farmers busy in the fields, up at the crack of dawn.
Poppies - cornflowers swaying in the breeze
Primrose and bluebells underneath the trees.

With Medieval churches, abbeys, cathedral tall
Ringing out their welcome the bells still chime for all.
Gloucestershire is a place, steeped in history of bygone days
Open to all who care, loving the country ways.

*Norma Collins*


## DEAR TONBRIDGE, YOURS FAITHFULLY

Dear Tonbridge,
        It's true, we are often confused,
With our prosperous neighbour of Tunbridge Wells.
The difference runs deeper, than just in the spelling,
Of an *O* for a *U*, this I'm sure you'd conclude.

With Tunbridge Wells, we sadly compete,
*We need a store like Marks and Spencer.*
But rivers we have and parks to be spent there.
It's a shame, yet we do, think we're incomplete.

The castle's improved and gives us all stature!
A history, our roots, with he-ral-dic crests.
We long to be worthy, and thought of the best.
For today's town folks, does this all really matter.

We are a small town and alive; a community.
But, modern day problems, do come our way.
A castle's no good, for holding this sway.
From all inner city ills, that we share some immunity.

In Tonbridge you'll find us, just as we are.
Astride the Medway, come see as she flows!
The town that spells it's *U* with an *O*,
Lying five miles north, from those wells, in a spa.

*Ralph Stott*

## CHRISTMAS IN PEVENSEY

Sitting near my window lit by candles
Orangey glow of fiery coals - Christmas music playing
But hearing outside the roaring, windswept gale
My mind races back several centuries to
An autumn landing of organised stealth
To avenge broken promises and promote a thwarted ambition
Magnificent William, ruthless, proud and systematic.
Has landed. England you'll never be the same!
This Norman will take your language, churches, people
And imprint his own immortality here.
White towers, villains, vassals, Domesday book and perfect arches
Are all part of his stamp of power.
Flying arrows, men's angry shouts - the fury of battle
Cut and thrust of swords - victors and vanquished
Together in a moment of time - fate favoured
William's grasping character that fatal day and on
Christmas day the conqueror claimed his crown.
Westminster Abbey witnessed ambition's reward.
25th December 1066, coronation of victorious Norman.

*Judith Moore*


## STONEHENGE

Awash with sparkling rain dust
She stood
In a halo of mist
She glowed
Beneath sun's filtering rays
She called
Radiating her mysteries in one surreal.

*Judy Gaskell*

## EASTBOURNE

So much variety packed into one town,
There's something for everyone. Why not come down?

| | |
|---|---|
| 5 minutes one way: | Browse through markets, arcades and shops, |
| | Visit the cafes, restaurants and clubs. |
| | Go to a film, or maybe a play, |
| | Then stop for a drink in one of the pubs. |
| 5 minutes another way: | A promenade and a scenic pier, |
| | The elegant beach; sea, sun and sand. |
| | Go fishing or sailing, paddle or swim, |
| | Or listen to music on the bandstand. |
| 5 minutes a third way: | Miles of downland with room to explore, |
| | For kicking a ball or flying a kite. |
| | Admire the famous breath-taking cliffs, |
| | Come for a stroll, or even a hike. |

Eastbourne, great fun whichever way you look at it.

*Tim Caroe*


## THE CROSS

A simple cross spells RIP
Three little words
One heartfelt loss,
Stands guard upon a promontory
In tangled briars and grass.
This sentinel of eternity
Chaffed by harvest winds
From vale and Clee,
Will murmur to all who pass.
It is I - I hold the key,
And watch over Worcestershire
This ripe county, jealously.

*Catherine Jones*

## THE VILLAGE POND

Whatever season of the year,
        The village pond will still appear
A lovely rustic country scene,
        Amongst the meadows, emerald green

In winter when the frost is white,
        The skaters glide, steady and light,
While underneath the icy rink
        The sleeping fish will barely blink

The water comes to life in spring
        With reeds, lilies and everything,
Spreading their life both far and wide,
        As moorhens make their nests inside

The early summer sun reflects
        The green leaves and coloured insects,
A willow's overhanging limb
        And fish bubbling around the rim

A regal swan glides softly by
        Beneath a peaceful English sky,
While dragonflies in green and blue
        Complete the gentle summer view

The autumn leaves of gold and brown
        Surround the water with a crown,
While misty boughs their sorrow weep
        By contemplating winter's sleep

***Doug Thomas***

## PAST AND PRESENT

Sussex by the sea, Sussex by the sea,
These words are uttered round the globe,
We're famous for our pots of gold,
Steeped in history, of battles and kings,
Of knights in armour; oh! So many things.
We've had dukes in their castles and flint mines deep,
We've even got our own breeds of sheep.
The Downs stretch out, with grasses and trees,
Rolling over countryside with the greatest of ease.
There are church spires standing so very tall,
Majestically towering and surveying all,
We've harbours and airports and much more besides
Miles of sandy beaches, the ebb and flow of tides.
Sometimes windy from the off shore breezes
But our weather down south very rarely freezes.
The summers are best with the warm sea air
Sussex is the only place I'd live; let's be fair!

*Carol O'Connor*


## LIGHTS ON OLDHAM EDGE

One night while trav'ling high o'er Thornham Top
I stopped to wonder at the sequinned sprawl
of myriad lights on night's black velvet cloth
now purple edged with promise of the dawn.
Aloof, above this glitt'ring spangled sea
strung out so long and bright like children's beads
are lights atop a distant hill unseen
that pale and fade as night's black pall recedes
and then, like fires of gypsies' late night meals
they die, as on the Edge the daybreak steals.

*Scott Richardson*

## MYSTERY TOUR

Leaving Worthing hospital, just the other day,
I had to take an Access bus upon my homeward way.
Whilst searching through the time-table, the first one passed me by,
Which meant a 20 minute wait - 'Oh well, that's life,' said I.
Now I have never travelled on an Access bus before,
So when the next one came, I tried to get in the front door,
But that door wouldn't open, so I tried the next, and soon
Was seated with my ticket in the bus that afternoon.
I had to get to Southwick Square, 'twas not so far away,
A 30 minute ride or so, if there was no delay,
But when we reached the roundabout, instead of going on,
The bus turned right for Shoreham Beach, where I have never gone.
We went around so many roads that I quite lost my way.
Were we going east or west? I really couldn't say;
I thought the sea was on my left, the harbour on my right,
I peered out of the window, but it wasn't very light,
And turning round the corner, to my surprise I found
The sea was right, the harbour left, the other way around!
At last we reached the High Street, then turned and went inland;
Some people left, some more got on, but no-one had to stand;
And when we reached Old Shoreham Road, instead of going east,
The bus turned west, which I thought very strange, to say the least.
We went up hills, along the roads, and then came down again,
Until at last we came up to the lights at Kingston Lane,
Then down Cross Road and through the square where I had
Wished to be;
I quite enjoyed my mystery tour - and went on home for tea!

*Hilda Brown*

## MEDWAY TOWNS - SO PART OF KENT

Within my time I have set foot
In many lands both near and far
Now years have past I've made my root
In dear old Kent, loveliest none bar,
Kent has it all, for all to see
A host of beauty, cities and towns
And county dear you're best for me
Your castles, orchards, fields abound.
So, for my life I shall then give
Devotion to this county fair
And 'til my end I'll always live
In Medway's towns - there's three towns there.
And in our towns such history
Now Chatham dockyard, fresh honours give
As new named Chatham maritime, but warships free.
Nearby our Nelson's memories live
Since Victory sailed from Medway to the sea
And close to the dockyard a unique castle lies
That's just a sham, near Upnors' beach
For close that place Dutch sailed to surprise
A lesson they did old England teach.
Then from our towns Charles Dickens hailed
And through his pen such stories read
Of Pip and Joe - e'en Magwich jailed,
Imagination our Charles did fetch
A voice of reason from the crowd.
So, finally from castle's top
Let's view the friendly towns below
And with the sunset's warm backdrop
Look at the place that I love so.

*C Saunders*

## EASTBOURNE, UK

E ach day I stroll along the front
A nd inhale the salty air
S unshine caressing all around
T o grace a town so fair

B ehold this place so pure and bright
O n almost any day
U nderneath the rolling Downs
R esplendent, all the way

N owhere else can be so nice, as
E astbourne, blue and green
U nless, of course, there's another town
K eeping everything pristine.

*J Power*


## OLD READING TOWN

The older we get the more we recall
Things that happened when we were small.
We swear our summers were always hot
And remember the love or smacks we got.
Old Reading's my best memory,
Reading Town as it used to be
Where my Granny lived near Whitley pump.
Given the choice I would always jump
At the chance to go and stay with Gran
And Grandad known as her *old man*.
Well that was sixty years ago,
Sadly things of the past must go.
New Reading Town is not for me.
I prefer to keep my memory
Of the brewery smell and the piggery,
Of chickens that clucked in Gran's back yard.
*New* Reading would make that very hard.

**June Marshall**

## ROUND CRANBROOK TOWN

Cranbrook's been my dwelling place for close on fifty years,
Pleasures I have had you know but there has been tears.
The Pound itself, for cattle then, at Willesley Pound Cross road now
Has changed into a roundabout, quite neat with lights that glow.
The Windmill next, a public house, the real one's round the turn,
It works you know and turns out corn if money you will burn.
'Twas built in 1866 at 72ft high and floodlight on some nights that lights up the sky.
Up you go to Bakers Cross, smugglers some will say, in olden days they plied their trade and then went on their way.
I live in Bloody Bakers house, tho', all the blood I find is from an old dead mouse.
Cloth Hall where weavers wore their cloth for people all around
Was next in line, before the graves of dead ones will be found.
The craftsmen cam from Flounders in 15th century time,
About the time of Edward III, who seems was next in line.
Then back we go towards the town that's lit up just for show
At Christmas time, when all take part and then on their way they go.
Up through the town when once there stood a jail, a cinema and a hall,
But now most everything goes up to Tunbridge Wells for all.
The school is one of many it has a Royal Charter found in Elizabeth 1st time,
She laid the stone of foundation for the school house standing by
It's altered now in every way, a grand hall reaching high.
Another school called Mary Sheafe stands beside the by-pass on wide and open lands,
I know I helped to clear the trees when it was just a lane,
The traffic goes rushing by causing quite a bane.
West of Cranbrook *years ago* is Glastonbury Park
Where at the end of lime trees lies deep down in the dark
A house, it was Napoleon's some of them will say
From the Battle of Waterloo, but some of them say neigh.
Full circle we have almost gone of Cranbrook, just for now,
Let's hope it meets with your request, with thanks to you, and how.

*H M Funnell*

## SOUTHWICK GREEN

There are two separate areas that fashion Southwick Green,
With a narrow roadway obliquely set between.
Oft has it been described, simply as common land,
It's very far from common! Some think it rather grand!
It really is a pleasant place with well-groomed greenery,
A fair and handsome show-piece, the pride of local scenery.
Shaped as a giant footprint, would rightly define the whole,
The lower green, the heel, the upper green, the sole.
Spacings in the railings were once wide entrance ways,
Allowing long-forgotten sheep their given right to graze.
Cricket plays a major part in the green's traditional mix,
Batsmen, of the recent past, sometimes, when hitting a six,
Smote it o'er the netting, set to catch each wayward ball,
And shattered tiles and windows of the nearby school.
Some citizens protested, all alleging dangerous play,
The council then imposed a ban, causing much dismay.
But Sussex people *won't be druv*, the cricket club stood fast,
Loyal supporters rallied round, recalling triumphs past.
In Parliament they questioned legalities and laws,
Famous personalities brought charisma to the cause.
Under threat of prosecution , bold batsmen battled on,
The ban was then rescinded, banishment was gone.
Summer sees Bank Holiday fairs and crowded charity fetes,
Bonfires blaze and revellers dance when nation celebrates.
On solemn occasion, as on each Remembrance Day,
The memorial sets a sober mood for all who pause to pray.
The old pond at the bottom has since gone down the drain,
The forge is now demolished, but swings and slides remain.
The scene is most attractive, as it has always been,
And still we have the freedom to play on Southwick Green.

*David Jackson*

**A TOWN FOR ALL SEASONS**

Enfolded in the South Downs' arms
Lies Worthing, town of many charms.
Where even on a winter's day
The sun is never far away.
And well stocked shops throughout the year
Make way for Christmas fun and cheer.

Spring comes early - gentle showers
Give life to multi-coloured flowers
With tulips red and daffies gold
A brazen glory to behold.
And grass is cut, and greens are fed
Ready for bowling games ahead.

In summer time, the town's alive
With coaches, and they all arrive
Bringing folks, all places from,
To stroll along the level *prom*
And have a meal, or see a show
Until it's time for them to go.

Here autumn, with its golden glow
Makes the approach of winter slow
And though beach games are out of style
Some visitors still stay awhile
And take a jaunt along the pier
Where anglers fish in water clear.

The people here are friendly too
And there is such a lot to do
To study and improve the mind
Or join a club - the social kind.
With all these things you will agree
That Worthing is the place to be.

**Elsie Anderson**

## SISSINGHURST CASTLE, KENT

Most die and leave
No contribution to the rest,
Some leave to others, like
V Sackville West.

In truth, herself a Tudor rose
To settle in the vision of her choice,
That where she walked - now flows
By breath of breeze the flower heads.

Reborn by hand of guided care
The setting for her garden gem;
Rebuild, restore, where need repair
The sad neglect of heartless man.

She understood what fed the soul,
What braced the urge of human kind;
Enhance by nature was her goal,
Revictual all of shallow use.

From ruins in their last decay
The gentle brush of effort swept
Till, like the dew's first light array,
Gleamed bright the gifts of nature.

Profusion of both sight and scent,
The feel of antique romance round
This greener spot in fairest Kent
Where song unpeopled breathes the tune.

The tune of nature dressed to show
The majesty of worshipped right,
Fused, harmonious, natural glow,
Rekindled light to long-dulled eyes.

What she bequeathed may we respect,
At what we see give lasting thanks
That time, forever here, protect
This aura of an English rose.

*Henry J Green*


## THE FISHERS OF ROSS

In Ross' gentle meadows close by Wilton's tower,
Many happy days we spend, close Vaga's rushing power,
With yards of string, jam butties, a jar or two of tea,
And silver fishes laughing as they pass us to the sea.

Early each morning, Harry, Bryn and I,
You'll see us walk these meadows loaded to the sky,
'Cause here we spend our holidays (a florin is the fee)
Who cares if Tommy Jones' hols are spent by the sea.

We've waited hours so eager 'neath Wilton's ancient bridge,
In raggy-muffin breeches, huddled on the ledge;
For the sparkle of a small catch - dull besides the glee
That lights our mucky faces, when the river's running free.

'Twas here by Ross' greensward we fished before *the call*,
My mates and I together, close Wilton's crumbling wall.
And those who will are grown now and still we cast a rod,
But Tommy Jones and Harry fish - some foreign sod.

To Ross' gentle meadows then when whispers up a blow,
You'll see the trundling fishers - faces all aglow.
And oft the stilly hour when creeps a new born day,
You'll hear their eerie laughter on the one-that-got-away.

*Jean Semple*

## THE CAPTIVE

It's many a year since I came to the west,
And I'd never thought to stay.
But fate it was that brought me
And I'm still here to this day.
I found such wonderful places
As I travelled in the west,
It was difficult to know
Which of them I loved the best.
I've seen the Roman relics
In lovely Georgian Bath,
I've dallied across Exmoor,
Walked Clovelly's famous path.
I stayed awhile in Bideford,
Had tea at Westward Ho.
Then later the Quantock Hills
And Taunton Dene I came to know.
'Oo be 'er? Where's 'er come from?'
I heard someone ask one day.
I told him, 'I be a furriner,
But I be 'ere t' stay.'
I never said a truer word,
For although I spoke in jest,
I knew I'd be held captive
By the magic of the west.

*Anna Marion-Cox*

**THE UNCHANGING SCENE**

The Ham with its backdrop the Malvern Hills
Is still nature's own cure for many ills,
A haven from the traffic and people's talk
And a lovely quiet place to relax and walk.

The grass smells as sweet on Tewkesbury Ham
As when I was much younger than now I am,
And the flocks of sheep are still grazing there
Where skylarks sing in the warm evening air.

The salmon still leap at the Severn Weir
Where the river's flow is strong and clear,
And the waterwheel turns at the Abbey Mill
Where the gentle Avon is flowing still.

I now see and hear many more powered boats
And even more anglers are casting their floats,
Yet the graceful swans still smoothly glide
And moorhens still nest at the river's side.

Lovers still stroll along through the grass
And they rarely seem to see me as I pass,
For the Ham is for them a private world
Though their love is just like a flag unfurled.

The sights I now see in the summer haze
Are much the same as in childhood days,
And though the town is busier than used to be
The Ham is still a peaceful refuge for me.

The Abbey bells ring with their joyous song
Across this meadow where I feel I belong,
A pleasure in store if you've never been
To this lovely part of the English scene.

*Roy Smith*

## BRADING DOWN

Climbing up the steepest road, engine labouring slow,
You reach the top and have to stop to study view below.
One can see for many miles, greenery and trees,
And, beyond their boundary at the beach, the sparkling of the sea.
Towards the west one sees the towns and villages entwined,
With farms and fields and meadows through which river seeks to wind.
And over on the western side, the stretch of countryside,
That meanders round the coastline from Bembridge on to Ryde.
And to the north one sees the same, with yellow fields of rape,
And, on towards the mainland, with Fawley's chimney shape.
At night the lights in distance, illuminate the sky,
And one can see for miles and miles, from this vantage point on high.
Surrounding seas of grey or blue, have upon their shimmer,
Lights of passing vessels that often wink and glimmer.
May we not take for granted this view afforded here,
Not everyone can see these things, so let's always hold it dear,
Or just drive uncaringly along the length of Down,
But see this mass of beauty and appreciate its crown.
This will help when daily lives are filled with anxious care,
For we know there is this calm retreat that islanders can share.

*C West*


## UNTITLED

Off the ferry, *Mountwood*, on to *Seacombe's* sunlit shore
Eagerly I step through memory's golden door
To pace again the prom and sand
With Mersey's waters lapping
And watch once more the tall ships,
Their brilliant pennants flapping
Past Wallasey's town hall, Mother Redcap's,
The Ferry Inn, Guinea Gap, Vale Park
With New Brighton on the horizon
And hours to go to dark.

***Ron Delacruz***

## WEYMOUTH BEACH

Sun shines bright upon the sand,
Sea twinkles with the waves,
Laughing children hand in hand
Enjoy these summer days.

Buckets and spades are working well
While parents laze and tan.
Sandcastles grow and trimmed with shell
To look the best they can.

Out there beyond the harbour wall
The yachts glide on the seas.
Maybe at *Lulworth Cove* to call
If they can catch the breeze.

While swimmers play and airbeds float
'Punch & Judy' call girls and boys
With shrieks they leave the balls and boat
Discard their seaside toys.

Sandwiches, with a sandy treat -
Even in the cans and drink
A feast that's very hard to beat.
An ice-cream now I think!

Then donkey rides, maybe a swing?
Or pennies in the slot.
We'll have a go at everything
'Cause Weymouth's got the lot!

*Shirley M Foster*

## CHAPEL CLOSE

High up in a sunny valley
Where once a chapel stood
Now stands our house in Corfe Mullen
Close by a shady wood.

*And in our garden half-buried
Lay local stone of red
Now wrested from the sacred ground
To edge a pool instead.*

There are few houses in our Close
But *peace and holy quiet there.*
Throughout the long and sunny days
Just birdsong disturbs the air.

*And if we walk out to the road
To look down Chapel Lane,
We'll see in grazing meadows
White horses with shining mane.*

To look across to Henbury
Upon a Sunday morn
A holy peace seems to be there
With the chorus of the dawn.

*At night when all is fast asleep
And darkness 'round is stood
There's just the sound of whisp'ring leaves
And owls in a shady wood.*

**Raymond White**

**RETIREMENT-VILLE**

Swing round the island, then straight down the road,
Take the left turn - into safety mode -
There's a gracious curve and a beautiful sight,
Trees on the one hand, homes on the right.

This is Retirement-ville, with all its delights -
The gardens immaculate - one of Dorset's great sights,
Where Grandma and Grandpa spend leisurely days,
Strolling down to the village, to enjoy local ways.

Take long walks with Rover right thro' the trees,
Sit on a tree stump and enjoy the late breeze.
Have a talk with a neighbour - he's a nice chap,
Then walk slowly home, to tea and a nap.

It's a peaceful retirement, they enjoy every day,
Except when the vandals come their way -
Then they creep back indoors till the danger's past,
And peer thro' the curtains - hope the torment won't last.

Then outside once more, to clear up the mess -
It's all they can do - we're beat, they confess.
Our lives here are peaceful, except for those louts,
With their language so violent and abusive shouts.

But the next day will dawn, as next days do -
And we'll still enjoy the lovely view.
This road is so pleasant, we must go out -
Let's show all our friends what life's all about.

*Mae Smith*

## CLOGGING UP MEDWAY!

There's chimneys smoking, people puffing,
Car fumes billowing, some folk huffing
Because they cannot get their breath
And greater, often, their distress.
The air in Medway's getting worse
Pollution is, a modern curse
I often read it in the paper
But to control it is a caper.

In local streets the traffic builds
From industry, some poison spills!
And bonfires weekly in back yards
No wonder we've got coughs, catarrh,
We're using tablets, puffers, sprays,
Trying to cure, unblock airways
The doctors say it's all the fumes
And how can we escape this doom?

Medway was once, a better place
But buildings continue to replace
All the little parts, once green,
Now bricks and mortar are the scene
And folk chop trees down in their gardens
Pour the concrete, wait to harden;
Those trees more oxygen were making
From the atmosphere - their taking.

Pollution is it masking all?
Change things now before we fall
We cannot carry on like this
Goodbye to life, we'll sooner kiss!
Medway, Kent is changing fast
Preserve what's good, let's make it last
Keep this England fresh and green
Each town, each hill, each narrow dene.

*Wendy A Cudd*

## BASINGSTOKE ALIVE!

Basingstoke is alive today.
Even Santa came with reindeer and sleigh,
The ice rink too gave a pantomime show.
In the evening massed choirs sang on ice you know.
The *partridge* flew over ice rink there,
*And twelve days of Christmas*, were skated there.
Then ended the show in a great display
As fireworks exploded in a wonderful way.

Fairfields school to which I was sent,
Now takes juniors only and an art school's present.
Many schools in the district now are found.
I hope they appreciate the education around.
So much of the countryside has now disappeared
But outside Basingstoke the fields are still here.
With the Field society we study the flowers
And wander the woods with bluebells for hours.

The *rejuvenated teenagers* 55 years and over
Have a club of their own where we talk things over.
We have speakers on subjects so diverse and many,
And outings and dances and parties for any.
So come to Basingstoke, there's a welcome for all.
The theatre and concert hall for you to enthral.
A brand new shopping centre's there. They've knocked down the old.
I wonder how people can be so bold.
We're the middle of south - the centre for all.
When you pass by - do come in and pay us a call.
Sometimes we go out, the transport is good,
We explore other towns, as anyone would.

***Margaret E Gaines***

## SWINDON

*Swindon*, a town in Wiltshire, where people are proud to live
Swindon, such a friendly place . . . where folk are pleased to give
*Fastest growing in Europe* - is the name that we've acquired
Yet even so . . . there is still . . . a lot to be desired!
Unemployment is falling, there's jobs to be had I'm told!
That is, of course, as long as you're not getting old.
Redundancies are slowing, but each one is a personal blow
Yet the folk of Swindon smile - not letting their hurt show
Marriages in Swindon hold the national high break-up rate . . .
Young lovers still make their vows - thinking that it's great!
Unwed young mums, with babe in arms, trudge to the social for help
Often leaving a puppy outside . . . so that it can whine and yelp!
A growing town - perhaps a city one day - that is our proud boast
Yet do we think of the homeless, the ones that matter most?
Homeless in Swindon . . . a fantasy . . . we've got no poor round here!
No down and outs, no cardboard homes, no youngsters living in fear!
There are some lovely bungalows, some wonderful houses too
Mostly with the curtains closed so nothing spoils their view.
Swindon was once famous, for its railway *yards* and trains
Now, if you should look around - little still remains . . .
There is a Railway Museum, a sight that recalls the past
Now that Swindon is a *high tec* town, wonder if it will last!
We have a wonderful hospital, there's Coate and Lydiard Park
A generous bunch of councillors - that charge, if you want to park!
Swindon has a football team, they've played against most of the best
They're even mentioned on Question of Sport: *who lost to all the rest?*
We also have the rolling downs, the Ridgeway, plus other delights
Wiltshire has the White Horse, Stonehenge and many splendid sights!
There is nowhere else I would want to live, nowhere, cross my heart
Unless I was offered a job in Wales, yippee . . . when can I start?

*Steve Clarke*

**WHERE ELSE BUT IN ENGLAND**

Where else but in England
Would you catch a carpet of snowdrops on a bleak winter's day
A posy of crocus' dressed in cream, gold and violet
Or bluebells nodding in jolly disarray . . .
Where else but in England
Would you listen with such glee to the Cuckoo's first song of the year
Or watch as ponies roam forests and moorland
Keeping their company with the fine fallow deer . . .
Where else but in England
Would you find scarlet coated horsemen
With hounds barking excitedly as they trail the red fox
Village fetes and gymkhanas sprinkled over the countryside
Where primroses give way to the tall hollyhocks . . .
Where else but in England
Would you witness such age-old tradition
The changing of guards, the trooping of colour with style
While Oxford and Cambridge row battle together
And the sport of kings takes place all the while . . .
Where else but in England
Could you enjoy the Henley Regatta
Drink champagne on a river bank, mark time with a favourite jazz tune
While the finals of Wimbledon take place on the centre court
And strawberries and cream remind you it's June . . .
Where else but in England
Would smacks of leather on willow evoke such a memory
Of cucumber sandwiches and hot strong tea
While church bells peel over the village and treetops
If heaven is thus, what a place it must be . . .

*A McFarline*

## FRIENDLY WIMBORNE

Have you ever been to Wimborne?
There's so much to see and do,
A fairly small, yet quaint old town
Waiting to welcome you.

In the centre is the Minster church
With chained library in one tower,
And a colourful model quarterjack
Who chimes bells on every hour.

See the museum and Heritage Centre,
Plus the model town's a good place to go
Built as a lasting reminder
Of Wimborne in 1-9-5-0 (one nine five oh)

We have many different breeds of ducks
And, most years, a swan family,
Plus some very proud peacocks and hens
Strutting round for all to see

So, as I said, we've much to see
Pubs, shops, parks, rivers too,
So do come and visit Wimborne town
Where a warm welcome will greet you.

*Ann Chambers*


## RIVER STOUR

Dear old River Stour, a silver thread
stitching Dorset's past to present time
always behaving like a thoroughbred
uninterrupted in your prime.

Through the night inch by inch you creep by
singing your runes, while all else is still,
Silver laden by stars of the sky
or shadow'd by each tall bosky hill.

Dear old River on your lonely round
you listen to lorn wind through the trees
and join the harmony of wind's sound
playing on leaves like piano keys

From your cradle-spring you flow alone
on through the Blackmore Vale, wide and free,
pausing to kiss the bridges of stone,
then, on to waiting arms of the sea.

***Aileen Hawkins***


**DORSET CAMEOS**

There is so much beauty in this Dorset place
Where heathered heathland meets the skyway space
As once it was in some far distant time.
And still in summer sun or winter rime -
Remains as timeless in its wondrous ways -
It seems the past is one with our todays.

And remnants of some mighty forest stand
As yet untouched by mans' destructive hand.

Here hedgerows guard the farmer's fertile soil
He serves the land as others once would toil.


The quiet streams and winding rivers flow
By towns and quaint old villages they go.

This then, the magic of this Dorset place
So blessed by God's divine and matchless grace.

***John Paget***

## DANCING LEDGE

When the Devil danced on Dancing Ledge
Such a hurricane did blow
That the seething sea, it hid the rocks,
That lay like teeth below.

When the Devil danced on Dancing Ledge
He swung a *wreckers* light
That pierced the gloom, like a star of hope
Through the dark and wild night.

The Master cried, as the rigging screamed,
'Helmsman! Bring the ship around!
By yonder lighthouse set our course
To Poole, where we are bound.'

The doomed barque foundered on the rocks
Her back she broke in two.
While the Devil laughed as the Captain drowned
And all the gallant crew.

His laughter rant to Peveril Point
And over Ballard Down,
By Studland Bay and Harbour Hights
It howled into the Town

Then the parson tolled the Longfleet bell
It rang through wind and rain
And the women knew their sailor-men
Would not come home again.

**Stephanie McGurk**

## MERLEY

It was but an urban village
With farmyards all around,
Within a mile of Wimborne Minster
Where so much history is found.

Then came along developers
Who saw potential there
And thus negotiated purchase,
And forthwith stripped the land all bare.

The new homes quickly sold,
Plots from plans selected,
And then this growing Garden Village
Into Merley was elected.

No longer an urban village,
Rather an urban town
With shops and schools and a mission church,
Minster chimes by wind carried down.

'Tis still a pleasant place to live,
Unspoilt by modern needs,
Where good neighbours still become good friends
With helping hand and friendly deeds.

***Leslie H Brown***


## MY TOWN

When visiting friends and relatives in some Lancashire inland town,
Strangers ask me where I'm from, I always get a frown.
I tell them I'm from Blackpool, they look at me sort of queer,
Then it's usually followed with 'What you doing here?'
Sometimes I feel they're passing judgement over some past visit made.
Perhaps they had lost some money, in a penny arcade.
But most times somebody cuts in, with a twinkle in their eye,
'Ee I had some good times there' then gives a little sigh.

***R Walch***

## FOSTER'S SCHOOL, SHERBORNE

In the pleasant town of Sherborne,
Nestling near the River Yeo,
Lay the School founded by Foster,
Way back in Sixteen Forty Two.

The Boarding House in ancient Fosters,
Set a model for all who came;
Dear Mr. Lush the cherished Master,
Respected by all, at School and aft'.

At start of War, new School was ready,
In Tinney's Lane with fields anew,
All pupils found the building handsome,
The Staff was formed by old and new.

4 PM on September thirtieth,
The war in action for over a year,
The bombs rained down all over Sherborne,
The glass at School all smashed and gone.

At last the final bell delivered,
Foster's success kept to the end;
Three hundred fifty years of caring,
Came closure, the end of Foster's dream.

Goodbye to Gibling, Miller, Lush,
To Welcher, Brown and Hume and House,
Our thanks for all you ever gave us,
The future lies in Gryphon's hands.

Old Fosterians, across the Country,
Led by McKay and Goode and House,
Are working hard to keep the memories,
Of countless years of proven worth.

*John Paulley*

## TYNEHAM VILLAGE

| | |
|---|---|
| T | The shock in autumn nineteen forty three, |
| Y | You all must move! War needs your village now. |
| N | No-one may stay - no child, no cow, no plough. |
| E | Each sacrifice by you will others free. |
| H | Huge doubts assailed them, fear took hold - |
| A | Asked courage stouter than was bid. |
| M | Many lost all but, buoyed by hope, they hid |
| V | Vexed feelings. When the war is won, they're told, |
| I | In faith you will regain your homes, your dues. |
| L | Look to the day. Forgo the happy school, |
| L | Leave fruitful fields, flowered woods and sparkling pool |
| A | And cottages deserted, empty pews. |
| G | Grave was that lie. None was let back. All wept. |
| E | England's great shame - a promise never kept. |

**Townley Shenton**


## UNTITLED

Nestled in the Primrose Valley you stand,
An elegant statue against the land,
Your ancient walls of cold, grey stone,
Tell of loved ones lost and those alone,
Your bells no longer make joyful sound,
Lest they fall and damage the ground,
But listen carefully, the rustling wind
Whispers tales to those who've sinned,
Thatch cottages rest within your sights,
And overhead the birds take flight,
The smile has gone from your face,
Lost in the twentieth century race,
What does your future hold,
Who will your earthen arms enfold?
*Clyffe Pypard Church*

**Heather Wannell**

**KENT**

There's more to Kent than just railways and roads,
Where wagons and lorries carry their loads.
The wonderful Downs run through to the sea,
To give us the white cliffs travellers see.
Wandering lanes where you hear the birds sing,
Lovely old churches with bells which will ring
Should this be too tranquil and you seek more,
Try Stelling Minnis where motorbikes roar.
Ancient woodcrafts too are there to be found,
Go gently through woods and look well around.
A man with a dole axe splitting a spile,
Or making sheep hurdles to his own style.
Watch *Folkestone Lassies* go by in full sail,
In the *channel* such clouds thrill without fail.
Then should you fancy a look at the sea,
There are miles of coastline most of it free.
The Hythe Dymchurch railway's a children's joy,
Though it is small it's much more than a toy.
The Dungeness trip's a wonderful run
And children all ages find it good fun
Where ever you go there's history there,
Which all the locals will willingly share.
Be it Biddenden Maids or Smugglers tale,
They're sure to know it almost without fail.
There's castles, houses and gardens galore.
And when you get there you'll find so much more.
I'm sorry to say I've run out of space,
Well at least it's been fun and not one lost face.

*W Todd*

**VILLAGE FETE (APPLESHAW)**

After the glare and din
of sale-stalls, big brass band
Childrens' races, funny faces -
I find here
within this large marquee
a hush -
a slower pace.
Here lie the prized jams and flans
the wasp-worried cakes and pies
arranged with tombstone precision.
Then shrouds of fine embroidery
an embodiment in a stitched
repro: of an artistic
idyllic way of life.
I see apples, blood red
and soft fruits, a red stain,
and earthed-up corpsed roots
laid out, their pain
watched over
in drooping prayer
by flowers with heady
funeral parlour scents.
These vegetables and the flowers,
some anointed with distinction,
are wilting in their exhaustion -
and in my admiration
as they lie there row on row,
I am reminded of the fact -
where they have come from
I will surely go.

*Gwynneth Curtis*

**THREE LOCAL VIEWS**

Wimborne Market, Station Road.
No more trains but stalls of trainers,
Printed T-shirts, eastern electrics,
Chinese junk.
Among the bric-a-brac
Unreliable second-hand cameras
And a stack of local postcards
Like a juke-box of old records.

The Post Office, Colehill.
The postmaster stands, Brunel-like,
Aggressively posed in front of *Cadbury's Cocoa*
And raw, red bricks, softened to sepia.
He bristles with Edwardian confidence
And walrus moustache.
For the rest, a horse-high signpost
Labels a deserted crossing of heathland tracks
And trees, trees, trees.

The War Memorial, Colehill.
Within its fringe of pines
A pale cross drips from shrugged arms.
A jogger treads water on the pavement,
Poised to cross the stream of cars
Flowing between banks of houses,
And a garage glows neon
Like a tank of tropical fish.

*Frank Pickering*

## DORSET NEWCOMERS

The sea, for me, is awesome and compelling because
I used to live more inland - now I've moved quite
near the coast.

The gulls, boat hulls, and lobster pots at Mudeford
being only a few miles from Ferndown is something
I can boast.

The gorse, of course, another change for us when
walking on Holt Heath and then around White Sheet
Plantation.

It's peaceful, natural, and so very quiet there
the silence makes us pause in fascination.

The theatres, none better, than in Bournemouth and
in Poole, in Ferndown, Wimborne and in other places
too!

The shops around, the parks abound, for us who've
just arrived and still exploring there is always
something new.

Retired? Inspired, is how we feel since we moved
to lovely tree-lined Ferndown with everything so
near.

The beach, within reach, the New Forest and Wimborne
Minster. We are at the centre of it all and really
love it here.

So here's a cheer for Dorset - it has an ambience
all its own and from now on it's where we will
always want to be.

For us, no more rush, just quietly settle here
and enjoy our brand new life poised between the
country and the sea.

*Sheila Beattie*

## CHESIL BEACH

Like a million diamonds sparkling on the sea.
As the sun shines down on its surface.
The gentle lapping of waves on the scree.
A hum of jet skis as they race.

Resonant plonk as a boy throws rocks
Happily into the water.
Cries of 'I can't find my socks'
Issue forth from my daughter.

Scuba Divers looking like frolicking seals,
Whilst they surface and submerge to explore.
A lad loudly exclaims, as in a fish he reels.
A motor boat zooms past, what a roar!

Smoky aroma of food from a barbecue nearby.
The setting sun glows behind a lone yacht;
Reminds me it is late and dusk will be nigh.
The children hint, dinner time, had I forgot?

*Sue White*



## PLACE NAMES

Five Lanes, Four Lanes, Threemilestone,
Playing Place, Shortlanesend,
Black Cross, White Cross, Red Post,
Blue Anchor and Lands End.

Scarcewater, Hayle and Stoptide,
Mount, Drift, Grade or Ley,
St Mellion, Mullion, Munions,
Loe Pool and Washaway.

Brighton, Rock, Row or Troon,
Brill, Flushing, Bugle, Looe,
Shop, Pity me or Come To Good,
There's Gweek and Redmoor too.

Search well and you will find them all
In the south west's furthest arm.
Visit them and discover
Just some of Cornwall's charm.

*Alan Potter*


## MODERN DORSET POET ANSWERS BACK

'So, this is where you do your writing?'
Glancing round my room they say:
Computerised and poised the lighting,
'Are you shut up here all day?'

They swear we work on empty bellies,
Need only air for food and drink:
Cry, 'Get yourself a pair of wellies,
Try walking in the fields to think'.

If slipping into well-filled ditches
Would they on poems concentrate,
With splinters bayoneting their breeches,
From challenging a five-barred gate?

Although we set computers pounding
Do not mock our useful Muse.
Some mute, 'Inglorious' are a-bounding
On desks of elm - or churchyard yews.

*V H Anderson*

## NEW FOREST NIGHTMARE

When all good Christians are in bed,
When night is black and moon half sped,
The Noadswood Nag awaits the time,
When wakened by the midnight chime,
Will race the heath and run the heather,
And chase all moon crazed things together.

The romp will start from Lady Cross,
And range wide over fern and moss,
Through bracken, scrub and leafy lane,
To Brockenhurst and back again,
To Bolderwood and Burley Soak,
To Anderwood and Knightwood Oak.

Then rushing on quite out of hand,
To Fritham and to Nomansland,
Through Stony Cross and Emery Down,
To Minstead and to Lyndhurst Town,
So end the Dizzy nightmare spree,
By Picket Post and Wilverley.

This madness lasts the full night through,
Till faintest daylight breaks anew,
Then, only then, he'll disappear,
And leave the forest pathways clear,
For any who are not insane,
To walk in safety once again.

*Doug Gregory*

**FROM HERE YOU CAN SMELL THE BREWERY**

In the leafy shade of the towns South Walks,
The old man listens as the old girl talks,
Up above in the boughs a pigeon squawks,
    From here you can smell the brewery.
In the ancient circle - Maumbury Rings,
The young man laughs as the young girl sings,
Up above the hawk seldom flaps his wings,
    From here you can smell the brewery.
In the Borough gardens on a summer's day,
Mothers chat whilst their children play,
Then happily while the day away,
    From here you can smell the brewery.
On the station platform, awaiting the train,
Locals and tourists, all the same,
To one another they oft' exclaim,
    From here you can smell the brewery.
Cows chew the cud in Dorchester fields,
Lush Dorset grass makes for good milk yields,
The pigs in the piggery chortle and squeal,
    From here you can smell the brewery.
In the busy streets of the old market town,
The shoppers bustle up and down,
The traffic travels round and round,
    And from here you can smell the brewery.
One industry in Dorchester is never in doubt,
There's one thing we in Wessex won't go without,
And from our bars the patrons shout,
    In here you can smell the brewery!

*Rosemary Price*

## A DAY OUT IN BLACKPOOL

Breezy Blackpool, sits on the Fylde Coast,
the North's top resort, is the proud boast.
Take a lift up the Tower, what a wonderful sight,
to see all below you, sets your senses alight.
Into the Ballroom, for afternoon tea,
followed on by a walk, on the prom by the sea.
Or perhaps, you would like to do it in style,
and take a *Landau,* along the *Golden Mile.*
Pubs, clubs, and shops, in endless profusion,
people selling their wares, amidst shouts and confusion.
Maybe something quieter, before it gets dark,
head out of town, to the famous Stanley Park.
You can sail on the lake, or visit the Zoo,
whatever you want, there's plenty to do.
But the best time of all, in the darkening nights,
is taking a tram, and viewing the *Lights.*
What a breathtaking sight, for seven miles,
people alighting, faces wreathed in smiles.
Wending our way, to our humble abode,
we'll have fish and chips, and *One for the Road.*
Home once again, and we all agree,
that dear old Blackpool, is the place to be.

*Margaret Wilson*

**LAKELAND PRIDE**

Oh the perfect lakes and fells
The land I know and love so well.
Calls to me when I depart,
it is the place that holds my heart.

It wraps itself around my soul.
Then cleaves to me and tightly holds
a portion of my inner side,
That craves the places free and wide.

Wondrous vistas fill my eyes,
How I love this perfect prize.
Oh the lonely changing hills
Where wild winds roar, or all is still.

The misty light on water shines.
Walls of stones that march in lines,
along the valley, field, and farm.
This chequered view brings peace and calm.

Though I may travel far and wide
I always remember Lakeland pride,
and soon return to my own place
and turn my face towards the lakes.

*Susan Bell*

## ON RIVINGTON PIKE

Up on t'Pike where fresh wind blows,
When Spring has melted Winter snows,
Lift up yer heads and fill yer nose,
With gradely moorland air.

Get up there where heather blooms,
Leave behind yer stuffy rooms,
Yer fact'ries, dark and dim as tombs,
Where there's nowt but work and care.

Stand on top, and look around,
A bonnier sight can not be found,
These moors are God's own hallowed ground,
For all of us to share.

Water's sweet in bubbling spring,
Hearken how yon skylarks sing,
Know what joy to t'soul they bring,
There's treasure there to spare.

Step along with merry stride,
Troubles never can abide
Where skies are big, and blue, and wide,
And gloomy days are rare.

Watch your worries slide away,
Such a gift and nowt to pay,
Would make a sinner want to pray,
'Cos heaven's up there - I'll swear!

*Eric Holt*

**BAITER POINT**

       It was the scene
Of many minor tragedies:

Once, a child's ball,
Caught by a gust of wind, skimmed,
Light as air, across the water,
Fading from sight at last amongst
The trees that fringe the island.

And once a terrier,
Its hunting season done,
Scampered, unleashed, into the waves,
Reliving for a moment its old strengths,
Nose lifted to the wind as if to scent
Some long forgotten quarry.

The cabin cruisers gently swing about
As the tide turns; and on the shore
A row of upturned boats suffice for seats,
Where many contemplative hours
Bring visions dancing on the waves
To eyes unfocused, dazzled by the light,
Of far-off scenes of youth and consequence.

Each step I take recalls another time,
Where we would dig for bait or rake the sand
Searching for cockles as the tide turned back
Leaving small pools abandoned on the shore.

And now, as then, the indifferent sun looks down,
Who's seen it all before, and will again.

*Dorothy Davis-Sellick*

## WOODSEAVES, HEREFORDSHIRE

They lay at the end of the forest
A cluster of huts formed of wood
Providing a home for the families
Who laboured and farmed for their food.

The forest afforded good shelter
For wild boar and deer at their best
But de Braose and the Baskerville owners
Pursued the wild beasts without rest.

Those two noble families weren't friendly
And often resorted to law
But agreement was reached when the town's end field
Formed their border in 1264.

They hunted and hawked with their nobles
And shot with the bow and used spears
Following a long day in the forest
They feasted and wined with their peers.

The boar would be roasted for hours
By the massive hearth fire filled with logs
And that left at the table not eaten
Was tossed with good grace to the dogs.

The villeins and serfs in their wood huts
Ate not like their lords every day
But an occasional hare or pheasant
Surreptitiously fell their way.

The fertile red soil of the district
Has long since been conquered by plough
Through the reason of popular edict
Townsend field remains extant now.

Today it's the parish boundary
Marked by hedge and cider trees high
Of rural historic old Eardisley
And bountiful Whitney on Wye.

*William Austin Pugh*


## A LIVERPOOL TRIOLET

Wistfully Wallowing by our Well-known Waterfront
The outline so familiar,
The spectres of a bygone age
wistfully wallowing by our well-known waterfront.
They share my space, my thoughts of maritime splendour.
The salted air that breathes nostalgia grips us,
wistful wallowing by our well-known waterfront.
The outline so familiar,
Liverpool, a city of pride and culture
a past and future all combined.
Architecture of an affluent age makes;
Liverpool, a city of pride and culture.
The aspiring peaks of the Anglican Cathedral, the beacon of St. John's
The mythical birds that guard o'er the city, sit on golden domes.
Liverpool, a city of pride and culture
a past and future all combined.

*Barbara Gillett*

## THE HALCYON SOUTH

The New Forest with its ancient trees,
Wild flowers, butterflies and bees.
Its famous ponies and fleeting deer,
All beauty and all life is here.

Glorious sunsets across Christchurch harbour,
And Mudeford Quay, where fishermen labour.
The Needles and the Isle of Wight,
Old Harry Rocks, a wondrous sight.

Bournemouth on a winter's day -
A path of silver sunlight across the bay.
The Solent and its graceful yachts,
The liners sailing to faraway ports.

Salisbury with the tallest spire,
And Romsey Abbey and its choir.
Winchester Cathedral with the longest nave
And Southampton, through the blitz so brave.

Beaulieu River and The Test,
Where salmon fishing's at its best.
Great manor houses and their estates,
Picturesque villages, where even time waits.

A halcyon place, with so much to do,
Walking, swimming and boating too.
A gentle climate - the south's often sunny.
Truly a land of milk and honey!

*Heather Rayner*

**THE ISLE OF THREE LEGS**

The holiday season has now begun,
Everyone's talking of having some fun.
Eagerly looking at brochures and travel books,
Where shall it be, camping, hotels or tree shaded nooks.

Let's take the boat to the romantic Island,
That lies between England and emerald Ireland.
Explore Castle Rushen and enjoy strawberries and cream,
Walk in the Fairy Glen to find the man of your dreams.

Witness the sunrise over the Plains of Heaven,
Then have tea and scones at half past eleven.
Join in the singing at Kirk Braddon on Sunday,
Shout for the TT riders racing on Monday.

Smell the aroma of kippers while smoking,
See all the herring boats coming and going.
Take the train to the top of snow capped Snaefell,
Drink in the beauty of hills, dales and dells.

This Island is magic for all the young people,
Friendships end up in a church with a steeple.
It's a beautiful Island and no other can compare
With the Isle of Man and its folk lore so rare.

*Eve Clucas*

## A LANCASHIRE PARTY

We're having a Lancashire party
In other words 'a bit of a do'
Inviting all of the family
And friends, some old, some new
Our Irene she'll make the trifle
Put sherry in too if she can
The liquid refreshment is well taken care of
When put in the hands of our Stan
The cake will be made by our Mary
For this she has quite a flair,
But her recipe is all a secret
So, she'll make it when nobody's there
The house cleaned from top to bottom
With no bits of dust left about
Is there anything we have forgotten?
'Don't think so' somebody shouts
At last the day dawns and we're ready
All scrubbed up and looking our best
The home brew is quite something this time
We know, it's been put to the test
The house soon is rocking with music
The children all dance in delight,
Friends smile and nod and comment
'Aye, it's a good 'do' tonight'
Then suddenly silence is called for
Not a sound, just silence descends
As Grandad asks, 'Please raise your glasses'
As we remember absent friends.

The party it then continues
Goes on late into the night
The old songs, generation to generation
All sung with gusto and might
The break of new dawn and it's over
And sadly we all must part
But the warmth of the Lancashire people
Is locked firmly within our hearts.

*Elizabeth Powell*


## WET NORTH WEST!

The rain it raineth day and night
I long to see the sun so bright
But clouds roll in so dark and grey
To bring us rain another day.

I watch the forecast on TV
To see if there is sun for me
In the south there will be sun
But for north west there will be none.

A migrant from the south am I
And yearn to see a clear blue sky
I am not used to so much rain
I'm getting water on the brain.

I do admit the grass is green
The best that I have ever seen
But what a price we have to pay
The rain it raineth night and day.

*Jenny Golds*

## MUNCASTER CASTLE

As I sit here on the terrace
With its glorious view of the hills,
My spirit is uplifted
And my heart with pleasure fills.
The castle has its treasures,
Beautiful and rare,
But the beauty spread before me
Is quite beyond compare.
Rhododendrons and azaleas
Provide a glorious scene,
Their blooms like jewels, glowing
Bright amidst the green.
There is no rainbow in the sky,
No daffodils below,
But the memory of this scene
Will never from me go.

***Barbara Kemp***


## LANCASHIRE - NOT AS BLACK AS

Enveloped by an air-polluted sky,
Covered by those famed *dark satanic mills,*
A cuisine of well-beloved hot pot pie
The birthplace of a nation's woes and ills.

We're known as the black spot of our country,
Land of clothe caps and Coronation Streets,
Folks say there isn't anything to see -
That clear blue patches are the rarest treats.

But they should come here and get acquainted
There's more to towns than historical parts.
They'd learn we're not as black as we're painted
For under the surface there's golden hearts.

***Sue Gerrard***

## LANCASHIRE

Blackpool, Preston, Burnley too,
Places, memories, all for you.
That is, if you read this ode,
Otherwise it's all in code.

Lancashire twang is very old,
As is, tripe and trotters, I've been told.
Famous people, an' Bandits too,
A bloody high Tower for all to view.

Butch Cassidy of Bandit Fame,
Or Cromwell's cave, another name.
Weaving sheds in Cotton Mills,
Lancashire lasses in cotton frills.

Cobbled Streets and Coddy muck,
Big Shire Horses to pull a truck.
Brasses shining in a hazy sun,
Kids with tops, having fun.

Hopscotch chalked on old stone flags,
Shiny black coal in hundredweight bags.
Canals and Barges, mucky paths,
Old iron bedsteads an' long tin baths.

It's almost gone as I grow old,
Romance of childhood, should I be so bold.
Good or bad them there old days
Soon to be a long passed phase.

Lancashire I'm proud of you,
I'm a Preston lad through and through.
I'll spread your stories far and wide,
Lancashire always in my stride.

*Jim Bland*

## CHESHIRE IS HOME

Cheshire is peaceful,
Cheshire is calm,
Cheshire is home to many a farm.

Cheshire has beauty,
Cheshire has love,
Cheshire has surely been blessed from above.

Cheshire gives life,
Cheshire gives relaxation,
Cheshire gives inspiration to a broad imagination.

Cheshire shows nature,
Cheshire shows rest,
Cheshire shows England at its very best.

Cheshire makes happiness,
Cheshire makes sights,
Cheshire makes all wrongs into rights.

Cheshire looks serene,
Cheshire looks grand,
Cheshire looks the best in the land.

Cheshire feels respected,
Cheshire feels together,
Cheshire feels great, whatever the weather.

Cheshire needs appreciation,
Cheshire needs care,
Cheshire needs attention, so as never to wear.

All of this, Cheshire is, but mostly it is,

*Home*

**Helen Johnson**

## LANCASHIRE LIFE

I live in a village, a Lancashire village,
There's a town that is really quite near,
It's been here a long time, you can read things about it,
There's booklets explaining the happenings here.

I live in this village *it's quite unimportant*
There's four churches, public houses as well,
A main street down the middle with shops and a post office,
And some old-fashioned cottages where people still dwell,

Just look at this village, it's really quite shabby,
Although there's new housing to see,
In the summer there's plenty of lanes to go walking,
Take bread for the ducks - how pleased they will be.

I know it may seem that this village is slumbering,
But there's excitement for someone each day,
It's life in the slow lane, and some people would hate it,
But it really suits me - so I'll stay.

*Eileen Lloyd*

**BROADSTONE**

Still called *The Village*,
Though now a small town.
Broadstone in Dorset
Never gets you down.

Stroll down the Broadway,
Plenty there to see.
Friends meeting, greeting,
Chatting cheerfully.

Walk in summertime,
Or sit by the trees.
Still scent lavender
Wafting on the breeze.

Winters are balmy,
Rarely does it snow.
Sometimes smell the sea
When the mild winds blow.

See the fine details
On the tapestry.
Telling the story
Of its history.

Still called *The Village*,
Though now a small town.
Broadstone in Dorset
Never lets you down.

*Patricia Thomas*

**DORSET LANDSCAPE**

Undulating hills give protection
To verdant valleys there between.
Gauze like mists above the meadows
Allow a glimpse of Emerald green.

A riot of rainbow colours
From rapeseed and of wheat.
Whilst 'neath the patchwork quilting,
The chalk hills gently sleep.

Over the winding Ridgeway
Nestles Weymouth Bay,
With water turned to liquid gold,
Kissed by the Sun God's rays.

Strong tides meet at Portland Bill
Lashing the rocks below.
As sea gulls wheeling, calling,
Keep watch on the ebb and flow.

This is Hardy country.
This is my place of birth.
Dorset an inspiration,
A treasure beyond all worth.

*Christine Llewellyn*

## NORTHERN EXPOSURE

My city provides
A meaty swim
For an interesting dip
Come 'ead and jump in
To add to this clue
Here's what I'll do
I'll give you some *Help*
Full hints you can muse
Cathedrals - we've two
Universities the same
We're west of the north
And have sea faring fame
Singing insects
A song struck river
And down to earth warmth
Put the meat in our liver
Business and pleasure
Give a hard day's night
If you've guessed Liverpool
Then good on you, you're right!

*S Armah*


## KERNOW (CORNWALL)

Scrumptious, meaty pasties
Whose aroma fills the air,
Delicious scones and home-made jam
Pint of 'Scrumpy' if you dare
Beautiful unspoilt scenery
Clean golden sands
Crystal clear blue waters
Cornwall, a blissful, idyllic land.

*Sandra Austin*

# KING COTTON

Our parents were cotton folks,
Now nearly extinct,
For winders, and warpers,
No longer we think.

Go down to the factories,
In clogs and in shawls,
With buzzers, to call them,
To hurry them all.

To get to the factory,
Before 'tgates are shut,
Thus losing a days pay,
Being locked out.

The children left,
With their Grannies at home,
The older ones playing outside,
With wip and top, and ball.

Those were the days,
When King Cotton was boss,
Yet I can't see that it's any great loss,

For Cotton fluff killed you,
Got on your chest,
Ruined your lungs,
Laid you to rest.

**Edith Freeman**

## THE RAILWAY UMBRELLA

Don't let it be just a story,
Told from someone's lips,
Of the Liverpool Docker
It's seamen, and their ships.

With Liverpool sea tradition
Why not from the past re-new,
The worlds finest overhead railway
With the greatest dockland view.

High above the waterfront
The train it ran for miles
And the sights of all those ships
Had everyone beguiled.

Families of seafarers, and dockers sometimes said,
'It's just like an umbrella that railway overhead',
Mile upon mile of sturdy railroad track
Even Gerry bomber flying through the flack
Couldn't break the spirit, of the men who called you wack.

Forget the Albert Dock awhile
And build some tracks and a train with style.
Lay them high as in the past
So we will have again
A Railway unsurpassed.

*E M Fogel*

## ULVERSTON - THE TOWN

Life was very different years ago when we were young
One of the jewels in the Lake District crown was little Ulverston
Small and neat with cobbled streets, even quiet it may have been
But being young then it's so easy to recall, so many different scenes
Railway lorries on the cobbles, shire horses big and strong
Rattling their way down Market Street, through a busy market day throng.
Who'll remember Captain Greenwood the Bellman of the town?
Peaked cap and walking stick, the bell in the crook of his arm
Stopping at each street corner, to give forth with 'Oyeh Oyeh'
To let the town know the happenings, that were taking place that day
Fair days twice a year were always such a treat
We ran to meet the Traction Engines, puffing up Fountain Street
From there into the Gill, where the men worked hard and long
To put the stall and rides together ready for the Fair Day throng
The smell of Hartley's Brewery, brewing beer twice a week
The trumpeter on Market Day King Street, the notes so pure and sweet
This then was Ulverston in between the wars
A wonderful town to live in, who then could ask for more
The post war years brought changes, a new road has split our town
New housing estates, new factories are scattered up and down
But all so pleasantly situated, so nicely camouflaged
The town beautiful as ever, though still not very large
Our sons and daughters left, to travel down life's road
The first thing to greet them on their return is the monument on Hoad
It seems to guard the town, it stands so straight and tall
Built in tribute to a famous son in 1850 I recall
Later would come others, a Queen's counsellor, two VC's
Even a comedian who found fame across the seas
This then is the history of our charming little town
New and old a perfect match, as night comes quietly down.

*N Ronson*

## ASPECTS OF THE INNER CITY

The belt is drawn tighter
And the fighter is born.
Loves can be torn
In our Wonderful City,
It seems such a pity
How the wind stirs the dirt
And people are hurt,
When we could work together
And weather the storm.
Where is the harm
In trying?
But it's no use denying
The Facts of our Life,
Where we stifle our needs
And give in to the Greed.
Are we really that cruel?
Are we fooling ourselves
When we say:
'It's a pity,
But it's the fault of the City?'

**Heather Render**




## MY ISLAND
*The rhyme of a come-over*

I came, I saw - you conquered, lovely Isle!
You took by storm my country-loving heart
With clean clear air and rocky streams that start
On purple moors and drop through many a mile
Of Glens to linger on the sand a while;
Fuchsia and gorse, challenge to painter's art,
Cottage and farm; folks never far apart
Nor far from music, meeting with a smile.

You ranged big guns, loaded with history -
The fossil elk, the barrows, runic stones,
Keills and castles, forts beside the sea,
Celtic and Viking, Scots and English bones.
You took me captive, lovely Isle of Man.
Here I shall end, though elsewhere I began.

*Lorna Viol*


## ORMSGILL RESERVOIR

Once a sanctuary for water fowl
refuge to weary house wife
ornithologist,
fisherman and the like;
the reservoir
is no more
a place of beauty.

On the bottom of the waters
shaley and lined with stone,
old tyres bask and slumber
between the supermarket trolleys
and old telephones
like the Leviathan monster.

Polythene tatters
hang gaudy from the trees
ingratiating themselves into the flowers.
While all around is the smell
of decay
and gas from the local towers.

*Ayelet McKenzie*

**ENGLAND FOREVER . . .**

From the very peak of Scotland
To the beaches of Cornwall,
Let the watery seas caress
This little island called our home.
Now London is our capital
It sits very proud and grand
In the centre there's the Midlands
Called the Industrial Land,
And Wales is renowned for its greeness
Very pure and true,
That's why I want to share
This beautiful island with you . .

Yorkshire is our garden
Full of hills and dales,
Our island is full of mystery
And unforgotten tales,
The potter's wheel keeps turning
Making china in a town called Stoke,
This place is named the Potteries,
Once embraced in a blanket of smoke . .

Canals our main source of transport
Built in the early days,
By hard men called the Navvies,
That made the British Water-ways,
But now we have cars and motor-ways
Trains very slim and fast
Our family and friends who lived miles away,
Are our neighbours so near at last . .

Dover is a colourful place
With the whiteness of its rocks,
But the thing we could not do without,
Are our very well known docks,
Liverpool and Southampton
To name but only two,
We say a hearty thank you
To the ships and all their crew . . .

***Ann Lander***



## WIGAN CARNIVAL

Come to the Carnival. Come to the fair.
There are baby shows, dog shows and side shows. See her
Attendants surrounding the Carnival Queen,
As she drives through the town in her fine limousine.
The floats are all following, look everyone,
- The procession is coming, isn't it fun!

Come to the Carnival. Come to the fair.
There are bookstalls, plant stalls and tents selling beer.
The Carnival Queen is really a beauty,
All year *for charity* she'll be on duty.
But while opening this, and opening that,
She'll always have time for a smile and a chat.

Candy floss, ice creams and hot dogs to share.
There are *Glamorous Grannies* - with newly permed hair.
A tent serving food, and raffles to win,
So much to see, but where do we begin?
Let's follow the band, everyone will be there
At Wigan Carnival, at Wigan fair.

***Dorothy McDonald***

## WIGAN MARKET

The naphtha flared which hissed
When, just a lad,
I ran around the stall-decked cobbled square,
Blaze in my mem'ry.
How I've missed
Trips with my Dad
To see the wares that were on offer there.
The lino rolls;
The china bowls;
The carpet strips;
The fish and chips;
*And mushy peas*,
Performing fleas;
Your fortune read;
The cut-price bed;
The cure for ills;
The purging pills;
The thick peg-rugs;
Enamel mugs;
The china dolls;
The folderols.
Oh where, dear market,
Have your traders gone?
You're just the long ago,
My happy *good-to-know*
Now dwells upon.

***Thomas Arthur Pendlebury***

## POULTON-LE-FYLDE

When the magical touch of a frosty night
enchants the trees and rooftops white,
and lingers a while, in silence adorning
the slumbering peace of a new day dawning,
I sometimes wish I might have been
born to a different age and scene,
and softly the echoes of days long ago,
come stealing to life in a legend of snow.

When the fish stones rang to the cries of old
and the coin of the realm was made of gold,
in the jingling, tingling morning air
by the ancient cross in the village square,
I listened to the wandering minstrel's song
and joined in the hustling, bustling throng
that filled the streets from far and wide
on a market day in Poulton-Le-Fylde.

*Frank Turner*


## AT LAST

We've been to many places
And seen so many sights;
We've known so many faces,
So many harbour lights.
      It seemed we'd never find
      That elusive 'peace of mind'.

It looks as if we've found it!
It could quite well be here.
Suddenly the pieces fit
In sleepy Gloucesterhire.
      That final harbour light
      Is coming into sight!

*Cecil R Bradbury*

## THE SAUL STREET BATHS

The dragon shrills the whistle
Flesh, white and wet
Emerges shivering, dripping
Like haddock from the net.
Jelly bodies.

Slamming the thick wooden doors
At pains to conceal their identical contours.
Hair darkened and uncombed, towelled
Into spikes, dipping into tin mugs
Of hot Bovril.

The bus moves off - snatches my memory
I see debris, the rubble, decay.
Saul St. Baths has had its day.

*Christine Meredith*


## THIS WILTSHIRE LIFE

The woods, the hills and the green, green grass
The local lads and the village lass
So quiet, no trouble this country life.
Clean fresh air, no rush and tear
Friendly locals everywhere.
Lovely views down Wiltshire lanes
The valleys we like to see again
Walking in a summer breeze
Birds singing in the trees
Thatched cottages, gardens of flowers to see
No hustle, bustle so carefree
Yes! It's the Wiltshire life for me
Inside or outside, sit, walk or ride
It's lovely in the Wiltshire countryside.

*I Sainsbury*

**UNTITLED**

As I ascend this Pennine hill;
A captivating prospect I behold.
This desolate region so grey and still;
Whilst the mill chimneys rise stark and bold.

Dreary is the weather,
As the raindrops tumble down.
Lustrous is the heather;
Though the swarthy storm clouds frown.

I would dwell nowhere but here;
In this domain, my spirit is found.
Nothing is so desired and dear,
As this sweeping; joyless mound.

The terraces that bleak and gloomy stand;
Are murmurs of the forgotten years.
The purple heath stirred by Summer's hand:
Subdues my plaintive tears.

The mist will shroud the moorland vast,
It will extinguish my sight.
The reminders of our industrial past,
Slowly fade with the approaching night.

In this dismal realm does my soul delight,
In the vale, where the tempest does moan.
The crescent orb will succeed twilight,
Under her beams I shall rove alone.

Vanquished is the eye that discerns,
This wilderness beneath the moonlit dome.
For intensely; fervently; eternally the heart yearns:
And this secluded Northern fell is my home.

*C V Nally*

## A DAY IN THE LAKELAND

Easy, it is to hop a train
Wending far away to the hills.
Relax! Watch dreamy views pass by;
Trees waving from their rocky sills

The train grinds in; disgorges all,
'Twixt Orest Head and Bowness Pier.
Then dash to catch the Mountain Goat,
And drive hard-by Lake Windermere.

Waterhead, Clappersgate, Skel'th Bridge,
And on towards Lake Coniston.
Close by cool lake shores, there to stop.
The Old Man looms to challenge one.

Onward, upward, ascending high.
Where sheep meander hills so free.
Amongst grey rocks, fair heather, where,
Lambs nibble food close by a knee.

The summit reached; then rest awhile,
To soak in all great glories there.
And loiter on 'twixt earth and sky,
'Til sun sinks slowly down to earth.

Time passes; one must leave behind
Such beauties that are free and wild.
A doubt once set in consciousness
With daily life is reconciled.

Scurrying down the Western slope,
By Goats Water to old Church Inn.
There to sup on a glass of gold,
Then homeward 'tis toward smoke and din.

*Máire Cowley*

## DENT FOOT CHAPEL

There is a little chapel
Along a Dent Foot Lane
This is where I used to go
In sunshine, and in rain.

Outside were a flight of steps
Inside were snow white walls
It was so meek and humble
But answered to the call.

We sang the hymns
We knelt to pray
To me it seems
So far away.

The Ministers and lay men
All lived round about
And Ella played the organ
For years I have no doubt.

Outside there is the old stone mill
Now silent with its age
By its side the river flows
So often in a rage.

So farewell my little chapel
I too am very old
All I have are memories
So well I do recall.

*Daisy Cooper*

## A SATURDAY NIGHT AT HOME 1949

Liverpool born and Liverpool bred,
Six in the house and two to a bed.
A sprint to the toilet
In the cold back yard,
When the snow was falling
Life sure was hard.
But never mind,
We've got the warm coal fire,
Though there's not much heat
Through the fire guard's wire.
Whose turn now to throw on coal?
The fire's dying - bless my soul!
Hey there you! With your knees all red,
If you won't fetch coal then go to bed.
Get the loaf out, let's have toast.
The one who makes it has the most.
The fire now is really hot
As fast as you toast, they scoff the lot.
Never mind, I've got the crust,
And for curly hair they say it's a must.
Shush! The radio's on.
Listen before the battery's gone.
'We three from Happydrome,
Members of the BBC,
There's Ramsbottom, Enoch, and me.'

*Peter O'Keeffe*

## CASTLESHAW ROMAN FORT, SADDLEWORTH

Majestic fort, standing calm and still
Enforcing on people its mystic will
Men have bowed to your overwhelming power
Trembling like a wind blown flower.

Your soldiers all rest in sleep
Silent in their tombs so deep
Only the breeze anoint your wall
Where sheep bleat with moanful call.

Your hidden secrets now overgrown
The moss cascading from the stone
The grass now growing green
Where once your power was felt and seen.

What scene of mystery would unfold
If your hidden heart I could hold
Strange powers from your soul so deep
Have made the mighty warrior weep.

Is your spirit really cold
Amongst all the decaying mould?
Is there life in your breast
Awaiting to arise from eternal rest?

Roman Heart at Castleshaw once beat
To the sound of marching feet.
Where Roman Sandal first trod
Archaeologist now walk your grassy sod.

*Peter J Wren*

## DEE ESTUARY IN APRIL

A sky of the softest delicate grey,
Gleaming skeins of water on glistening sands,
A frosted silver sea, and over the river
A long dark line of mountains far away.

The hard black whale back blurred with driving rain,
And then was gone and everything was lost
In a pearl afternoon of gauzy showers, but then
The mist ebbed and light flowed in again.

And gorse flamed on the sombre grass once more,
Until again the sea was bare to the drifting
Dance of the showers, and the pale lilies
Of daylight faded and died on the lonely shore.

A flurry of fine rain swirled in from the sea,
Was cold on my face; and suddenly you were not
There, with me, watching the evening shroud
The desolate sands and marshes of the Dee.

You were out of reach, gone, beyond the bay
Far as those lonely lights, along the Welsh Coast
Leaving forlorn the rain and the dusk and the wet grass,
And I was sorrowful, human, half away,

Where ever you were, and the dusk and the estuary
Slipped from my hands, and all the power to stand
And see entire, was gone and I was walking
Sadly in the rain by a darkening sea.

*John Clifford*

## THE NEW SPIRE ON STOWMARKET CHURCH

It was a bitter cold February day
The temperature was way down low
The sky was grey and overcast
We even had a little snow

It was early on a Sunday morn,
Usually there's no one about,
But in our little town that day
So many people had turned out

The cranes arrived at break of day
The streets were closed and traffic free
All stood gazing toward the sky.
What was it they had come to see?

For nearly twenty years our church
Had been without its spire, so tall
Workmen had to take it down
Before it should collapse and fall

Now, there beside the strengthened tower
Was the new spire, copper clad and bright
On top a gilded weathervane
It was an awe inspiring sight

And so the great day had arrived
When our church received her graceful spire
The crowd looked on as, slow, it moved
Then gradually rose up, ever higher.

When lifted to its final place
The spire, which had stood so tall
Upon the ground, now raised on high
Look tiny as it towered over all.

*Elizabeth Cook*

## WATERLOO KEG DAY

Waterloo Keg Day is coming soon,
It falls on Sunday the eleventh of June.
What it commemorates I haven't a clue,
It's just an excuse to have a good do.
Bacup Town Centre is full all day long,
Bargains galore, going for a song.
There's something for everyone, it's really a treat,
And bunting hangs on every street.
There's hot-dogs, toffee apples, candy-floss too,
So forget your diets and join the queue.
For the kids there's a funfair and bouncy castle,
You can look round the stalls without any hassle.
Some people turn out in fancy dress,
There's a dolly who's name you try to guess.
Side-shows galore where you may win a prize,
And a man who paints faces before your eyes.
So let down your hair and come along,
The finest people you'll be among.

*G Marshall*


## IN MY SUSSEX GARDEN

In my garden, tall and grand,
three weeping willow trees there stand.
Their slender, drooping leaves are found
stretching hard to reach the ground.

In my garden, wide and long,
the birds chirp out their merry song.
And every day at dusk and dawn
two squirrels play upon the lawn.

In my garden, at its end,
the river Arun snakes and bends,
and whispers as it passes by,
beneath the splendid Sussex sky.

In my garden, by the Downs,
a wealth of beauty can be found.
'Tis Eden recreated there,
a place on earth beyond compare.

*Stephen Gunner*


## MARDALE

Beneath the water, far below,
Where once were trees the fishes go.
And where the grazing geese were seen
Upon a quiet village green
Now speckled trout with watchful eye
Rise swiftly for the drowning fly.
The church bell's silent, gone the tower,
Clocks no longer strike the hour.
On hearthstones where the fires burned bright
There waves a rippling water light.
The village sounds have died away
No dogs bark, no children play,
No singing from the Dun Bull Inn,
No bird song when the days begin,
No sheep bleat, no cattle low
All is silent down below.
And far above the old hills lie
Their shape unchanged beneath the sky.

*Marion Jones*

## AQUAE SULIS

Midst city walls both tall and cream
The secret alleys: a tourist's dream.
In narrow lanes bedecked with flowers,
They while away the daylight hours.
And restaurants with china clatter,
Full of folk with happy chatter.
The city floor with traffic teems,
And intermittent sunlight gleams.

Here, Roman-sandalled footsteps trod,
Or rode a horse, with feet unshod.
Their countless legions crossed the sea
To build by pasture, lane and lea.
From then, for countless ages past,
A City grew, the finest cast.
And many of great rank and fame
Built homes in Avon's leafy lanes.

Then enterprising men like Nash,
Who set the fashion with a dash,
Who's entourage from London Town
Displayed the latest lace and gown,
Made Bath, this City from a crater,
A thing of beauty and far greater.
A place renowned throughout the west
To take the waters, sleep and rest.

Now tourists come from far and wide
To watch the sparkling Avon glide
Down the steps 'neath Pulteney Bridge,
O'er it's shallow man-made ridge.
And on folly-topped surrounding hills
The view, breathtaking, ever thrills
The visitor who stands in awe,
Upon the busy valley floor.

*Marie Bowerman-Taylor*

## THE FLOWER STALL AT BECCLES

They used to sell flowers at the crossing
Where the slow train to Norwich goes by,
Tight bunched sweet smelling violets
As blue as an Irishman's eye,
Spring time poises of primrose, cow slip and iris tall,
In mauves and purples and yellows, Dutch and English and all.
But today when I stopped at the crossing
Where the slow train to Norwich goes by,
The stall was deserted, the benches were empty,
I wonder why?

It must have been back in the eighties
The last time they set up their stall,
Carnations, chrysanthemums, cornflowers,
Daisies, delphiniums and all.
'I'll get some tomorrow,' I said to myself,
Watching the train go by,
The flowers would be there tomorrow,
Just like the stars in the sky.

But I never went back for the violets,
Seduced by the high street store,
Where they had them in paper and plastic and sugar
And feathers and fabric and more.
But the scent isn't there and the feel isn't fine,
And the blue isn't true, not at all.
So I went back today and the notice said *Closed*.
How I wish I had bought them before!

*A M Bowles*

## THE LANE IN TOWN

The squabble starts eight-thirty sharp
Drivers fighting for a place to park
Where do they all come from?
Where do they all go?
What is it that they say?
What is it that they know?

A private row comes through the wall
Though pretend we never hear at all
And say 'Good morning'
Trying not to pull rank
Then smile with pity
Knowing they have debts at the bank.

Neighbours dash out in a rush
All year, blazing sun and snows slush
With shopping in their carrier bags
And business documents in cases
Lives in a race with time
Tension and worry in all the faces.

So there's a hullabaloo, have no doubt
And we guiltily know what it's all about
A message from the church bell rings
Making dogs bark and howl
While the robin in the tree just sings
And the cat's out on his hopeful prowl.

But 2 am is a different time
When all is silent and done to mime
I can not hear, but see stars bright
In perfect peace the day times lack
Even the wind gives up his fight
The resting street mourns in black.

*K Scarfe*

## NEARBY TO LOUGHTON

Beautiful countryside,
long winding roads,
autumnal colours,
my pretty abode.

Farms with their animals,
fields with their crops,
birds of all sorts,
nest in endless treetops.

Fresh air and beauty,
lush forests hold peace,
folk tales and mysteries,
will never cease.

Dick Turpin, a legend,
rode brave through our town,
his hideaway cavern,
has raised many a frown.

Mystical churches,
like picture postcards,
stand old and serenely,
within pretty churchyards.

Lakes and long rivers,
are cool and inviting,
life is unveiled,
like a choir reciting.

I like where I live,
I have contrast and choice,
I am close to the city,
but the Essex side gets my voice.

*Carol Ross*

**ESSEX**

When I was young all the Eastend went
on *beanos* to Southend, heaven sent.
Miles out in Essex near the Estuary sounds
where fun and enjoyment, sometimes sunshine, abounds,
the beaches of mud when the tide went out.
The Kursal and the rides that made us all shout.
Cockles, winkles, jellied eels and Kiss me quick hats
old coaches, brown ale by the bucket and back to the flats.
For most of us this was Essex only seen
twice a year from a coach ride through countryside green.
Now I'm older I realise what the county has to show
in scenery, beaches and produce to grow.
I'm an Essex man now from head to toe
not many Sharon's or Tracy's do I know
the image created by TV and press
does no justice to the Essex I know and I guess
that always I will remember the earlier years
of Southend and the world's longest pier.
Wherever I travel no matter how far I roam
Essex will always be my place for home.

*Peter Hewing*


**A LITTLE BIT OF NORFOLK**

A little bit of Norfolk is in all of us I fear,
A little bit of Norfolk in all things we hold dear.
A smile, a glance, a warm embrace, the words 'How are you dear?'
Yes, a little bit of Norfolk reaches everywhere.

A little ray of sunshine is in us all to glow,
Yes a little lighted beacon in the darkness wholly shows.
Without this beaming candle, the world seems such a mess,
But a little ray of sunshine brings forth happiness.

A kindly friendly shoulder to sometimes lean upon,
A kindly friendly shoulder, it seems to right most wrongs;
A fleeting glance, 'I'm on your side', this problem we'll pursue,
With friendship right beside you, all worries you'll undo.

*Anthony Paul*


## THETFORD

Kings house was a hunting lodge
When James 1st was king
There are the remains of a priory
And old church bells still ring.

There was evidence of a Saxon town
When they excavated years ago.
And Thomas Paine was born here
As everyone will know.

The ancient house, now a museum
Shows off its 15th Century charm
From Tudor times the bell has stood
The ghost - it does no harm.

The conical shape of castle mound
Tempts children still to run around
Are there treasures once concealed
That have never been revealed?

Spring walks is a sylvan green
Where the river thet still flows.
Nuns bridges captivate the scene
As they did long, long ago.

*Daphne Flello*

## THE VILLAGE CHURCH

I know a village church
It stands just up a lane
Sometimes has brought happiness
But some times grief and pain.

Now many years ago
Our country was at war
The Germans dropped a landmine
In that church yard which made us sore.

When the mess was all cleared up
The grave stones all put back
They made a sunken garden
With roses and a sundial plague.

This church I knew so very well
Now after it was repaired
And hear the church bells ringing out
For this church that I cared.

Now in this church I married
It was a lovely day
And everything was beautiful
For that we had to pray.

*B Salter*

## CHANGING DARTFORD

There used to be swans in Dartford park,
Down by the river side.
Two goldfish ponds and a bowling green,
The Rose garden it's pride.
The market was held in Market street.
There were shops of every kind.
And the heath was wild and glorious,
Refreshing to the mind.
Trams, and a town steeped in history.
Cinemas full at weekends.
But if you wanted to go to Essex,
You took the ferry at Gravesend.

Now the tunnel takes you to Essex,
And the bridge brings you back.
Cinemas are clubs and Bingo halls,
Of shops there is a lack.
Dartford Heath is now criss-crossed with roads.
The market's held elsewhere.
The centre of town is modern and bright,
The trams no longer there,
Bright gardens now cover the goldfish ponds,
Cover the bowling green.
The park's Rose garden remains in bloom,
But the swans are seldom seen.

Some buildings are still steeped in history,
The church remains its pride.
Not all is changed, but you cannot stay,
Or turn back times changing tide.

*Irene Seager*

## ON THE DOWNS ABOVE SOUTHWICK

### EARLY MORNING

Here are gifts I would give you,
here on the quiet hill;
when the rest of the world is sleeping,
and the morning air is still.

I'd give you the gold of the autumn sun
touching the fallow field;
and the silver of the distant sea
so secretly revealed;

and the jewels of these moments,
so rich, so rare, so bright,
that I envy not the songbird
its singing nor its flight.

these are the gifts, the gifts I'd give you,
here on the quiet hill,
as the rest of the world is waking,
and the morning air is still.

*Chris Goodwin*




## PLUMPTON PLAIN DIG

It's not so many centuries ago
   That Ashdown Forest stretched to Plumpton Lane,
When Downs bore all the crops that man could grow
   And August's sun lit lynchet lines of grain.

Then, maze of tracks led from the fields to hovels
   Huddled midst bush and brush to shield from weather,
Within ditched walls hard dug with staghorn shovels,
   To keep from fox or wolf the beasts at tether.

So archaeologists infer: the sites
   On Plumpton Plain are mapped in Bronze Age guides . . .
But I think, Bronze Age ghosts haunt moonless nights
   And saunter to the scarp in spectral strides

To look on Plumpton in the Age of Plastic
And wonder at a culture so fantastic.

***E Westbury***


## WEST SUSSEX

Stately Arundel, her brown river
Flowing 'neath the castle tall,
Truly a most gracious giver
Of her beauty, over all.

Proud Petworth with its crooked steeple,
Quaint narrow streets and kindly people
As another gem of the Sussex Weald
To many a traveller has appealed.

Nestling 'neath the swelling down
Lies a little market town,
Steyning, with a smiling face
Shows a certain pretty grace.

But 'tis Bramber's tiny village
Which I deem the fairest part,
With quiet lanes and many a cottage
It has more than won my heart.

***Elizabeth Rodgers***

## A CENTURION ON SELSEY

As I marched along the coastal plain
As far as eye could see
I spied a jewel shining thro' the rain
Beside the tempestuous sea
'What is that place' I puzzled
And went my weary way
Each step an ache of muscles
My pack a load of hay
'Tis the Sea of Seals' was uttered in my ear
'A quiet rare and peaceful place
A sanctuary for man and birds and deer
Where once our foes held space'
'A sanctuary you say!
Rare indeed to find
In this unsettled age and day
An omen for our peace of mind.'
At this the sun God came to light
A ray of sunshine o'er the land
We turned as one towards the sight
Of azure sea and golden sand
We continued on the beaten way
Light of step and sad no more
Until upon the close of day
We came to gaze upon the shore.
A crimson orb now leaning low
Blazed a path from an isle offshore
'Welcome Sextus, fret no more'
I murmured to my friend,
We'll build to the North of this Seal Sea Shore
And live content to our journey's end.'

*Brenda Choppen*

**A TOWN OF RENOWN**

The beginning of Tunbridge Wells
Came about in a curious way
When Dudley, Lord North, in 1606,
Rode through Broadwater Forest one day.

A water spring gushed from the earth
The colour an interesting red,
North drank some and took home a sample
Saying it cleared his poor head.

'Medicinal waters!' folk cried,
'A holiday we will arrange!'
The rich and famous went to be cured
Of all ills from migraine to mange.

The well was fenced round for convenience,
Wooden shops were found to be handy,
Followed later by houses and coffee rooms
Controlled by Beau Nash, the town dandy.

The architect Decimus Burton
Was asked in eighteen-twenty eight
To lay out a park and some villas
Known as the Calverley Estate.

The tree lined walks near the spring
Where the whole adventure began
Was named 'The Pantiles' because
The bricks were baked in a pan.

Tunbridge Wells has beautiful churches,
Famed cricket ground, Rocks and great buys,
If Lord North could see the RVP
He'd fall off his horse in surprise.

*Frances Green*

## THE SOUTH

Butterflies dancing on the breeze
A meadow lark's faint cry
Daffodils swaying - make me sneeze
Chalk hills go rolling by.

A tiny brook goes winding
Cottages nearby
Sun rays shine on crocuses
To catch and please the eye.

The weather's always milder
Way down the south you see
It's warmer living here you know
Than by the cold north sea!

**Marina Roberts**


## KENT - GATEWAY TO EUROPE

It's called the *Garden of England*
As every schoolchild knows
Where apple trees and strawberries thrive
And where it rarely snows!

But for me it's the *Gateway to Europe*
Where I can always discover
An exciting, different lifestyle
No better, no worse than another.

Still, I'm always glad on returning
To catch sight of the white cliffs of Dover.
And inspired by the riches of Kent
Know adventurous days aren't yet over!

**Diana Cole**

# MY COUNTY

Sussex my county,
Sussex my home,
Soon I will return
If ever I roam.

East of the County
The cliffs and the sea
Downland and meadow,
It's all home to me.

The beaches and towns,
Small villages, too
The day that I leave
Is the day I will rue.

I love this place
Something always is new.
Round the bend in the lane
Another comes into view.

Its flat boggy marshlands
Stretch on for miles
Fields joining fields, linked
By a series of stiles.

Swans glide on the river
Crossed by a small bridge
A hawk hovers, then
Glides away, over the ridge.

From the top of the downs
You can see a long way
You want to sit and gaze
At the view, all day.

*Anji Tuppen*

## SUSSEX

Good old Sussex by the sea
Is not the place it used to be;
Just inland from the shore
The Towns have grown more and more,
So that 'the coast' is
A noisy megaopolis.
But don't surrender to despair
Go, seek the lovely Sussex air.
Leave the frantic towns
And cross the rolling downs.
There you will discover
Stunning views and leafy cover,
And many a pub and market town
Of ancient character and renown.
Working mills can still be found
On exposed and windy ground.
Old lanes, cut, into downland chalk
Descend in many a pleasant walk.
And dew ponds and chalk fed streams
Give food for thought and tranquil dreams.
These hills and valleys by 'men of stone' were known,
Although their domain was choked and overgrown.
Now the land is tamed and cleared
But still by 'Sussex Men' revered.
Many, by this lovely place, have been inspired
And have found the peace that they desired.
If you seek, you too, may find
That elusive peace of mind.
So wander 'off the beaten track'
And free yourself from the modern rack.

*Neville Croll*

## A WINDY DAY IN CROFT WOODS

The wild winter wind, through the stark stately trees
Echoes the rushing of white tossing seas.
Soggy brown leaves smell sweet where they lay.
And dried leaves are whirling and twirling at play.
Clouds hurry fast 'cross the steely blue sky;
In the wake of the wild wind, see how they fly.
The air is aspin, with the fresh breath of living;
Exciting and vibrant, taking and giving;
Testing the strength of small budding leaves
Chasing the sparrows to hide in the eaves.
The rough chilling wind, tugs now at my hair;
It's strong, and it's vital, and strips the trees bare;
Breaking dead branches, that snap 'neath its force;
Creaking the boughs, as it rushes on course:
It wails through the woodland, and whines through the bushes,
Rippling the fish pools, and swaying the rushes,
Croft Woods are thrilling, with gusty winds blowing
My senses are reeling, my blood is fast flowing.

*June Newton*


## DARK SIDE

Moonlight masking mysteries,
Murders, mayhem and tragedies.
Lurking under its misty air,
Feel the lull of its despair.
Skyline beams stretch afar,
Clothing for a naked star.
Whispering willows crackle in the dim,
Disguised as dreamers, deep within.
Sleepy light trickles down,
Demolishing darkness, the evil clown.

*Kathleen Clarke*

## ALL SAINTS, SHROPSHIRE

If saints have sprung from Shropshire soil before us,
As we have heard and read in days gone by,
Let lives in tune with admiration's chorus
Be lived, that their example shall not die.

Since Liber Festialis for his order
Was penned by Myrc of Lilleshall long ago,
God's grace has stretched His kingdom to the border
And saints on earth have seen that kingdom grow.

From Rowton, Richard Baxter rose to rapture,
And wrote of 'Saints, their Everlasting Rest'.
'Ye holy angels bright' his pen did capture
And mortal men his ministry has blessed.

To Madeley came John Fletcher, good news bearing,
From life of ease as chaplain to the Hills,
Where, like his lord before, his life not sparing,
He served 'among those dark, Satanic mills'.

When Hodnet's rocks had yielded crystal fountains,
Through Heber's loving labours and his hand
Wrote down those words, 'From Greenland's icy mountains,'
The Gospel echoed in another land.

Then How, in Whittington, with pen so gifted,
Wrote of 'the saints, who from their labours rest;'
And then that lovely 'O my saviour lifted' -
How Shropshire's soil with glory has been blessed!

So let the saints be ever recollected,
For all their words, their witness and their worth
And, in our lives, their spirit be reflected,
As we to this fair shire give glory birth.

***Bill Woods***

## EGDON HEATH

Thomas Hardy called it Egdon Heath,
I walk it often so know it well.
But what if its future nowadays,
I wonder! Who can tell?

At this moment in time it's hardly spoilt,
So it's a place I like to go,
Especially when, I climb to the top,
Of a heather covered knoll.

From here I see the beauty,
Of the countryside,
A green belt of my Dorset,
Stretching far and wide.

I never tire of this glorious scene,
From the horizon where I see,
The hills, the trees, the valleys.
A peaceful tranquillity.

The heathland, fields and forests,
There is beauty everywhere,
And I know that I am breathing,
The purest country air.

An ever changing landscape,
I see as I turn round.
And I wonder if I am privileged,
To be standing on holy ground.

And as I look below me,
I see my village and my home,
This is my part of Dorset,
From where I'll never roam.

*A Crabb*

## A PLACE TO VISIT

St Annes-on-Sea is the place for me
The folk who live here are swell
The ones who were born here are called 'sand grown'
And they have lots of tales to tell
Of days gone by before houses were built
On hills made of sand
Where cart wheels made ruts on the paths
On the prom a hotel called 'The Grand'
The gentry used to visit from near and far
By train in their hundreds
And now by car
It still has a fascination all year round
People come to visit and wander around
We're between 'leafy Lytham' and Blackpool with its lights
Pleasure Island and St Annes Pier will soon be in your sights.

***Barbara Froggatt***


## GRINSEL HILL

Calm, quiet rocks, pathways winding,
Heather purple, blackberry bush,
Tall trees waving, fireweed binding
Grinsel Hill, so green and lush.

We climbed, to reach a windswept height
Where we the open plain could view,
We paused, as clouds the sun's warm light
Assailed, with black and velvet hue.

Lone kestrel sailing on the air
Swift earthward fell in deadly calm.
Black beetle startled from its lair
'Neath dock leaves scuttled, safe from harm.

It seemed as if both heaven and earth
Stood still and silent, ceased to breathe.
Past and present, life, death and birth
Creation's glory did bequeath.

*E Balmain*

## CROFT AMBREY

Did Caractacus watch the wintry sun
Rising over Ambrey Hill,
And see the silent deer run
Through the woods so quiet and still?

Relics of oak woods still remain
Upon the Croft, with newer pines
Standing alien and dark, in rain,
With no memories of ancient times.

Did once a mighty river flow
Below across the plain
Where now the fertile fields grow
Summer crops of golden grain?

Where once a warrior king held sway,
Sheep and harebells hold their fast.
The Sunday bells of Aymstrey play,
And peace today belies the conflict of the past.

*M Checketts*

## WARRINGTON BOMBINGS

Weeping walls wash away the bloodshed
as the crippled are cradled whilst lying on the floor,
and madness rules as they take away the dead
and the peace campaigner's shown to the door.

Bleeding buildings bemused by barbarity
close their curtains and call out to us all,
to sit down and talk for a final solution
and stop banging our heads 'gainst their walls.

Now the street's deserted silence reigns it once more
until the same time next year on Remembrance Day,
when we sit down and kneel in the holes in the road
and to some higher authority we pray.

*David Geldard*




## THE CHURCH OF LOGS

The Church of St Andrew
The world's oldest made of wood
At Grinstead in Essex
For so long it has stood.

This Church it was a resting place
En route to a new shrine
For the body of King Edmund
Who was martyred back in time.

The split oak Saxon logs of old
Red Tudor bricks, porch and spire
Dormers of the nineteenth century
All are still here to admire.

*Kathleen Barker*

**LOST AND FOUND**

Going off to Southwold on a nice hot summer's day
Tried avoiding traffic, and then we lost our way
Decided to keep going to see what we would find
Traffic left behind us, so we did not really mind
Driving down the country lanes, Snape Maltings on the right
Surprised it was in Anglia, unexpected sight.
Kept going down this country road until we reached the end
All alone we travelled and turned a right hand bend
Not knowing where we'd come to, wherever could we be?
And then a sign made known to us, 'Twas Aldeburgh by the sea.
Now we have lived in Anglia for near eleven years
And yet the news of Aldeburgh had never reached our ears
Before our eyes, with pleasure, such beauty to behold
This place that we had come to was very, very old.
Walked along the High Street, found interesting shops
An inn upon the corner, near where the high street stops.
Turning off the main street, found little country lane
Which led us to the sea front, where old houses still remain
Ancient timbered cottages, one with balcony.
People having drinks there, had a view out to the sea,
Found a seat and sat there taking in the view,
Decided then that one day, we'd like to live there too.

*Anne Torrington*

## CERNE GIANT

Night with its crowd of stars, with its white star faces,
Far as imagined space, close as the touch of your hand,
Darkness thick as a shroud on the dying land,
And the wind roving the world like a restless tiger.

This is the ancient place, the haunt of the Helith,
A cry on the echoing air and blood on the grass,
Here, where the present holds the hand of the past
And the future waits for a day that's a long time dawning.

Here, where they spilled their seed on the terrible hillside,
Where they cut in the bone-white chalk this antique scar,
Where the shadows cluster and crawl in a nightmare of fear
And life grows cold as we wearily wait for morning.

Innocence come and gone like a passing stranger,
Terror and torment, rape and unwanted birth,
No-one to pity her, none but the angry earth
And the wind, roving the world like a restless tiger.

*M D Pike*




## OSWALDS (NEAR LULWORTH COVE)

If I let my thoughts run
To where I like most to be
It's on a remote Oswalds beach
With my dearest friends for company.

I sit and observe the scene
Which changes as I gaze
Cormorants perching on jagged rocks
The dancing sea reflecting sunrays.

Black headed gulls bob together,
They seem so at ease on the sea,
Waves crashing and pulling on the shore
Such sounds strangely comfort me.

Whether the wind is in tranquil mood,
Or blowing a gale on Oswalds bay,
I love to be there, to listen and see there,
Just as I did today.

*Devina Symes*


## A SPECIAL PLACE

On a spring morning, so long ago.
I went to this special place, where humans never go.
I was greeted by the woodpecker, who was on the tree
Then I saw the blackbird, thrush and starling they all chirped for me.
Along came the fox, badger and rabbit all happy as could be
Because this is their place, and that's how it should be.

On a summer's morning a year or so ago
I went to this special place, where the humans all now know.
I was greeted by a fence and gate, and all the trees were gone
A sign which said sold, to the road transport this land belong.
As I stood there with a tear in my eye
I felt so sad for my lost friends, to whom I never said good-bye.

On a winter's morning just like any day
I went to my special place, but it had gone away
In its place there's a carriageway, with traffic all the time.
Now I think of all my little friends, who's land they called mine.
I wonder is this progress, or a fault of thine.

*Roy Hawker*

## SHINGLE STREET MYSTERY

In summer, when the wind is not so keen,
And seagulls glide while skylarks sing above,
I never think of how it must have been
In wartime, in this peaceful place I love:
Where all my true contentment I derive.

But now in winter I believe the tale
Of blazing sea and dead men on the shore:
Their voices in the moaning wind make wail,
Their restless spirits haunting ever more
This lonely place where they were burned alive.

Was it a blunder tragically made?
Did British soldiers meet their death by fire?
Or were they Germans hoping to invade
That perished in that salty funeral pyre?
And in the carnage, did a few survive?

To gladden hearts of parents, or a wife?
Returning home when peace was won at last
So thankful for a second chance in life,
And eager to forget the dreadful past,
With memories too painful to revive.

Perhaps at night they live through troubled dreams
Of rubber boats afloat in sheets of flame,
And, waking, hear their fellows' screams
As, agonised, they call out someone's name,
And call on God their troubled souls to shrive.

And now it seems to me I hear their cries;
Or is it just a bird tossed by the storm?
I call myself a fool to fantasise
And, curled up by my hearth so safe and warm
I hear my husband's footsteps on the drive.

*June Trelawny*

**ESSEX LIFE**

Prehistoric Essex so primitive and wild
From many civilisations its present life was styled.
In a densely wooded region, first signs of life began
Around the Clacton area for early Essex man.
These food finders and hunters struggled, but survived,
Living standards improved, when foreign farmers arrived.

The New Stone Age had started and although progress was slow
As more people came to settle, trade began to grow.
Fine flint tools and weapons, pottery making skills,
Artistic decoration of daily utensils.
Their rough and ready workshops, when the Bronze Age came to be,
Produced ornaments and weapons of notable quality.

The introduction of iron led to foreign trade,
But this success and wealth caused the Romans to invade.
Their technical ability and culture more advanced,
Meant life in ancient Essex was furthermore enhanced.
Roads were carved through woodland, colonies were built,
The birds eye view transforming into a patchwork quilt.

Four hundred years of Roman rule, then the Saxons came,
East Saxons settled here and hence the county name.
Their habits and their customs it's probably true to say,
Formed the very basis of Essex life today.
The Danes were next to take control, when the kingdoms were invited,
To join as one and so ensure that England was united.

Essex history from thereon was part of the national story,
County museums and trusts, protecting its personal glory.
If Colchester could only talk, what tales this town could tell,
Of those historic structures which within its boundaries dwell.
Essex is a county of ever changing scenes,
Of winding roads and rivers and ancient kings and queens.

*B M Mynard*

## NORFOLK COUNTY

N is for natural beauty, home grown food,
O is for 'oh you don't you be cheeky and rude.'
R is for regal and stately houses,
F is for falling over 'you've put your knee through your trousers.'
O is observing what's around you and keeping it in mind
L is for 'Listen hear you young ones learn to love and be kind.'
K is for kinship's friendly folks to meet.

C is for 'Come on in rest them hard worked feet.'
O is for oneness with all that's around and near
U is for undone shirt buttons and a clip round the ear
N is for nature, the rabbits, the deer, the riverside, croaking toads
T is for tractors and farmers with the harvest reaped loads
Y is for you know what I mean, the place with the bendy old roads.

*Kaz Holman*


## WHERE SHEEP SAFELY GRAZE

In Forest sheep may safely graze
But by the sides of roads they laze
And roam around the villages
Where some eat all the cabbages.

They are partial to flowers too
Will also mow the lawns for you
And tourists have to wait to pass
Whilst sheep in road eat tufts of grass.

They have no fear of motorists
Because they know they were here first
And claim the Forest as their own
It is the only place they've known.

Forest of Dean, where they roam free
And part of Forest history.

*Violet Croad*

## NORTH NORFOLK

North Norfolk is a place renowned
For peace and quiet all around.
Hunstanton in the North West lies
Brancaster from the sea doth rise.

Sandringham needs no acclaim,
Home for the Sovereign who doth reign.
To Blakeney Point, if that appeals
And take a trip to see the seals.

Now Blakeney is the home for boats
And anything in fact which floats.
And Walsingham to see we must
Where pilgrims go to in their trust.

Then on the marshes are the birds,
Where 'twitchers' go to, in their hurds.
A windmill's set in nearby Cley,
And Kelling. Weybourne are close by.

Now Sheringham's a pretty place,
When tide is out, there's lots of space,
Then Cromer is the next resort.
Where from the sea, the crabs are caught.

There's Holt, a Georgian Town Inland
With Gresham School, it's rather grand.
And so, No matter where you be
North Norfolk air is pure and free!

*B I Dawson*

## DURHAM MINERS GALA

Sturdy Durham Collier, his grievances to Durham, he takes each year
Yet not in a voice of anger, but in splendour, a sight without compare,
From daily toil beneath the soil, in unity they emerge
And from every Village and Hamlet, on to Durham City they surge.

In voiceful song they march along, each Lodge banner flying high
Preceded by local Colliery Band, to Durham is their cry
City, Cathedral and Castle wall, no longer stand to defend
But open wide their ancient gates, to welcome loyal friend.

Through every road and narrow street, by Old Elvet they congregate
From a balcony of Ministers and Leaders, to the silent mass they relate,
The merits of each speaker in turn, earns the right to represent
And from County Hall, the Miners rights to London will be sent.

From each side of the Wear, they wave and cheer, on route to the fair,
To see such happiness, and enjoyment, you'd think there was never a care
Laughter and song, persists all day long, with dancing in the street,
There's fish and chips, hot pork dips, and the pub where old friends meet.

Uniformed bandsman, again music blend, and play a hymn as the Gala
                                                                                                 ends
With banner held high, and Homeward bound, it rallies Village friends
Then this they all, proudly recall, their Democratic rights to be free,
Crusaded by Miners Champions, like Cook, Hardy, Shinwell, and Peter
                                                                                                 Lee.

*Gil Vincent*

**ESSEX**

East of London lush and green
With forest trees of oak and pine
A peaceful place a pastoral scene
Lies Essex on the Central Line.

Suffolk North and Kent lies South
And to the East the mighty sea
Thames opens up her gaping mouth
Letting all her water free.

Market Towns and busy ports
From countryside to shopping mall
Sandy shores - seaside resorts
Essex seems to have it all.

Country pubs with ingle nooks
All part of this mast shining pearl
BMW's East End crooks
And best of all the Essex girl.

The weekend brings them out in force
For checking out the social scene
To hunt down Essex Man of course
At the Castle down at Woodford Green.

For Essex has its comic side
The victim of the seedy joke
As Chigwell ladies pose with pride
While sipping on their Rum and Coke.

As London workers daily melt
To this tranquil County for their rest
If you live in the Commuter belt
Then Essex is the very best.

*T A Tuvey*

## FELIXSTOWE

Nestling in the country
Twixt two rivers and the sea
It's not the place where I was born
But still it's home to me.

There are cattle on the marshes
Wild birds in the grove
All kinds of craft out on the sea
As on the prom I rove.

Goods wagons on the railway
Cranes clanking on the docks
Seagulls wheeling overhead
In raucous, screaming flocks.

Migrating birds, some rare ones too!
Landguard fort, martello towers
Chattering shingle on the shore
Sea front gardens bright with flowers.

Beach huts for the 'regulars'
Day trippers by the score
But when winter winds are chill
Felixstowe is ours once more.

*B Smith*

## THE RIVER AVON
## WINDING ITS WAY FROM BATH

Fast flowing river now a swirling stream
In the heaving wake of a pulsing Boatman's dream
Mallards swim and circle wide
Gay and proud on the churned up tide.
Beauty enriches the rippling mass
As a kingfisher darts in a brilliant pass
Coots dive free from human sight
To rise again away from fright
Wild mink appear in mock surprise
With perky amusement in their eyes
Luckless wren caught in tangled strand
Close to the numbered anglers stand
Cormorant swoops in deadly dive
Fish too slow - does not survive
Cascades of water as both arise
Victor proud, with captive prize
Lusty lark sings to his kind
Lazy heron wings where the river winds
Dreams of Otter, instead of mink
There at the cut where the farm cow's drink
Damaged willow with boughs bent low
Impeding the current, and swirling the flow
Fascinating river of past fame and deed
Flowing by Sydenham's Mead
For here camped Lord Monmouth and his troops
Before his march to Sedgemoor, his life there to lose
Ageless river, used for game and leisure
To transport work and idle pleasure
Rippling and eddying through the years
Outliving man - and all man's fears.

*C Cottingham*

## AVON AURORA

I wake to find a swirly of mist
Over the fields,
Outside bleakness overshadows trees
And cold persists.

The dew hangs on the sobbing morn,
This world where clouds
Sit steady and at ease,
To watch the dawn.

Here is all flatness - but there a hill
Beyond,
Rises above these dreaming spaces
Where life is still.

This place is where the cows lie,
Dozing quietly,
And a slow warmth spreads
As sunlight bathes across the valley.

*Julia Hemings*

## EVENING ON WATCHET BEACH

I saw a triangle upside down filled up with layers of the bay
like the tubes of coloured sand we found on the Isle of Wight:
A wide silver sky stretched tight and light across the day
touching too soon a sea that was losing its blue.
Pebbles lay hard to shine the night time beach
where a child emptied sand from her shoe,
her gold hair blown on the air
beyond the rocks and the pool
where a drab little crab
kicked out his legs
brown and swimming
and infinitely
alive.

*Barbara Hine*

**GLOUCESTER CITY**

Gloucester, City of my birth
Accepting me,
As I grew, so did my love
So free.

Gloucester, City of growth
Encouraging life
Giving me hope, developing
Without strife.

Gloucester, City of change
Dynamic climb
Watching the men cut into your crust
Sad time.

Gloucester, City of roads
Networks black,
Men crawl all over your earth
Resist look back.

Gloucester, City of Survival,
Concrete jungle,
It hurts to see you this way,
Gigantic bungle.

Gloucester, City of money,
Name progress
My countryside sacrificed for this,
Sad mess.

Gloucester, City of Joy
Shining through
Cannot stifle beauty so rich, whatever
Men do.

*Heidi Bevan*

## WEOBLEY

Weobley is a village of around a thousand souls, several shops
a doctors, dentist, two schools, a vets, slaughter-house, three
places of worship and a vicar for each day of the week.
It has much that is of architectural interest, being considered
by many as the finest black and white village in the country.
The houses are constructed of an oak framework infilled with brick
or plaster, many of which contain such great age their walls bulge
into the very streets.
Other smaller cottages stand in short rows, stooping and round-
shouldered, some prevented from falling by a single piece of wood,
their owners (clearly of the same habit) can be easily identified
as you walk the streets of this pleasant village.
The church, who's impressive spire can be seen for many a mile
is of red sandstone and very big.
Its financial condition will be found to be of the same colour and size.
Groups of new houses stand a respectful distance from the old and
in the main are of little interest, being red-bricked, detached and with
little character.
Some villagers believe this also to be the case with their owners.
The residents are a mixed lot, there being a small number who's roots
lie within the village, but in the main most are incomers.
There is much commuting by those of working age, Hereford twelve
miles, Leominster eight miles, but many are of older years and for
them the village provides a place where much retirement can be
enjoyed.
Most of the inhabitants will be found to be of a pleasant disposition
and prepared to exchange pleasantries should you decide to visit this
village and gain something of its charm.

*Tim Barnes*

## CIVITAS IN BELLO ET PACE FIDELIS
## (CITY FAITHFUL IN WAR AND PEACE)

The Cathedral rises up from the banks of the Severn,
A Mecca for the pilgrims or perhaps their seventh heaven
The promenaded history is a riverside mystery.
And the boys who secretly carved their names in King's College walls
Probably gave their lives in the two world wars,
Only to have their names carved again in memory,
By the very men who taught and caned them.

Now Edward Elgar, Worcester's most famous son
Looks across a busy College road,
At a symphony of car exhausts in carbon monoxide mode
A crescendo of noise as the rush hour moves in
A masterpiece of combustion percussion that could have
been composed by him.

Jellied eels are on sale in the old market hall,
Next to the butchers and the dairy produce stalls,
But fishing and the fisherman's trade has long since gone
Now Worcester sings only to the potter's song.
The river and canals used to be arteries to the old City heart
Now railways and motorways have taken over that part.

In New Street, by the old City walls,
You will find King Charles' pub where he escaped from the
Cromwellian wars.
Justice, Plenty, Peace, Chastisement and Labour -
The five guardians of old stand over the Guildhall chandeliers
and gold,
As the council that presides within,
Discuss which part of Worcester's history is next to be sold.

Oh, Worcester, Worcester, walled medieval city of old,
Your history wasn't won cheaply, so at what price is it to be sold.
Oh, City faithful in war and peace,
Is it black tears or pears that the castle keeps?

*David Ind*

## AVON, MY HAVEN

I'm just a simple country lass, who leads a simple life
I love to walk on a summer morn
Through harvest fields of ripening corn,
I love to roam through Midford to the Castle on the hill
Coombe Hay down in the valley then on to Tucking Mill
I love to walk high on the hill and hear the squirrels chirr
The pewit and the curlew, what memories they stir.
The perfume from the hedges, from clover fields and tare
A walk along the river bank, my thoughts still linger there
The black bird and the skylark singing their summer song
I hope to find a four leaf clover that I can wish upon.
These are just the simple things that I with Avon share
And say a simple thank you Lord, and hope to linger there.

*Rose Anderton*


## DEAN HOME

Little cottage, made of stone,
amid the trees of Dean.
Blackbirds sing with muted tone,
the grass, an emerald green.
Whisper trees and cry you sheep,
all along the Haine.
Peace and serenity, will you keep
'til I come home again?
Look down across the Viney here
and see the fields all sown.
Breathe in the fresh and heady air
and know the joy I've known.
Though I may wander far away,
on foreign soil may roam.
When I return, I come to Dean
and this cottage, made of stone.

*Heather Geddes*

## TO THE VISITOR OF HEREFORDSHIRE

Keep it to yourself
Leave the brochures on the shelf
Be a little vague, a little circumspect
And deflect
Any pointed questions about your holiday
Just say
Something noncommittal
About the place you have been and it'll
Be alright. The very secret, secret just
Must
be kept a little longer
For nothing could be wronger
than for everyone to know about our county
so beautiful and bounti-
ful. It belongs to us you see.
We're assimilating strangers but only gradually
and we need a few more years
to dispel our fears
of hordes and hordes of trippers -
Mums and dads and nippers
cousins, uncles and aunts
Traipsing through our county pulling up the plants
(I know they wouldn't really, but it makes the rhyme)
Such a wondrous county if you've got the time
to explore it gently, going at our pace
Largely undiscovered still with lots of space.
Don't fill it up with visitors. Don't speak its name out loud
Just keep our little secret so you won't be a crowd
And if pressure's ever put on you
Answer 'I really didn't see much. I was only passing through'.

*Stan Pinches*

## THE LEGEND OF ESSELIE (ASHLEY) CHURCH

David Kenric was his name, Shropshire standard bearer proud,
Riding south to serve Black Prince and join the army loud.
The knight so bold through forest rode until he lost the way,
But then the squire found back the path, at Esselie that day;
In 1346.

The knight was pleased, raised his spear and threw it hard and low,
'On that spot I'll build a Church' he said, 'that is my vow'.
'If God spares my life in war, to Esselie I'll haste back',
Then with his retinue of men he rode on down the track;
In 1346.

King Edward and his son Black Prince, with English army large,
Raised banners high on Crecy field, French soldiers there to charge
They won a famous victory, back home they came in glee,
Amongst them David Kenric, riding north to Esselie;
In 1346.

His vow he kept, and now it's known, the Church indeed did grow
Out of that spot he marked that day when spear he did throw.
And still above the village proud stands Ashley Church today,
With changes many since that time, but here always to stay.

*M Haslehurst*

## THANK YOUR LUCKY STARS

E mbedded in the County it seems since time began - lay the
V ale of Evesham through which the River Avon ran:
E ach meandered turn reveals enchantered new delights of
S trawberry fields and orchards of every fruit you like.
H istoric Towns and villages from thatch to Cotswold stone it's
A mazing how many people flock here to pick-your-own
M oreover, the surprise the amount of veg that comes from out the ground!

V isitors pull up by the coachloads to buy our vinegared preserves,
A sparagus, apples and cider, too many it may sound absurd, for
L ocal or 'home-made' seem to resident folk the norm, but then
E vesham often takes for granted, beauty and fortune with which it's born.

*Gill Ricketts*

## THE RIVER SEVERN

The Severn it flows in the valley below
Forming a horseshoe, so winding and slow.
But fast flows the Bore ride now in the Spring
As o'er nearby meadows the seagulls do wing
Yes, fast flows the Bore with high crested wave
Bearing debris and branches, and rushing so brave.

Bringing the ocean way up through the fields
Bursting the bank as it crumbles and yields
Swirling and whirling its way from the West
Of all England's rivers the grandest and best.
Greyly meandering its wintry way
Or shimmering there on a warm August day.

Through meadows green of a lush, lovely land
Past cows coming down to the edge of the sand
Past churches and hamlets, and orchard and town,
And a city of age-old name and renown.
Or, from the hillock now spangled with dew
It lends  fresh enchantment to the view.

*J Selwyn*

## THE MALVERN WAY

You feel the need to get away
For 'tis summer, the sun is shining
The weekend is in sight
And for fresh air you are pining.

But where to go, what to do
Can I make a suggestion and say
Pack a picnic, prepare a flask
And walk the Malvern way.

The Worcestershire beacons the challenge
(OK, you could lounge in the garden instead)
Nearly two thousand feet can look daunting,
And takes many a weary tred.

But there really is nothing like it
The scenery's a joy to behold
Man and nature side by side
As peace and tranquillity unfold.

The eye scanning o'er the horizon
The indescribable feeling of space,
One almost feels in a time warp
There's no rush, no hurry, no pace.

Just make sure you feel in fine fettle,
As the climb is no piece of cake,
And if you are feeling 'not quite fit'
Then the peak you may not make.

But even if you only get part way,
And find you have to stop
Praise yourself you got that far
There's always next week to get to the top!

*Heather Perrott*

## COLD FEET

I felt the spidery rush of rain
running from my linoleum hair
assault the still-warm sea of flesh
beneath my shirt. I didn't care.
I moved my feet to ease the cramp
and noticed that, despite the damp
how dry the pavement was just there.

I'd shivered now for two whole hours
waiting, patient, God knows why!
I wondered if you'd get away
from him tonight. I must soon fly.
And then it struck me - How obscene!
That passion hitherto could mean
for us not patches wet, but dry!

*David Clement*

## THE SEVERN BORE

I went with friends to Empney, near Saul
And there we all
Saw
The Severn Bore
A wall of water, riverwide
Preceded the tide
We were most impressed
To see on its crest
Young men riding the Bore on skis
All of these
Standing with nonchalant grace
A'top the Bore's foaming face
Showing that this natural wonder
Could not steal their thunder
Yet despite the marvels I saw
I found it a bore!.

*Joe Silver*

## HILLS OF HOME

When I saw the Malvern Hills I was just a child
Lost in wonder as I gazed, hillsides green and wild
Many years I roamed afar, in city and in town
Never did my heart forget hills so green and brown.

In my dreams they came to me, in every season fair
Outline of the lonely hills, towering high and bare
As the years were passing by, now I was fully grown,
To the hills I came at last, they are now my own.

Roaming in the hills each day, fair or stormy weather
Solitude I came to seek, treading turf and heather
Wandering over meadowland, Malvern Hills rose sheer,
Every shadow, cleft of rock, every outline clear.

Often when amidst the hills, in stillness and in calm
Here where I forget myself, finding peace and balm
Hills reveal to me the way along the path of life.
In the silence speaks a voice, far from angry strife.

When a child I loved the hills, leaving memories deep
What I glimpsed not understood, I was still asleep
Things intangible, unseen, revealed in many ways
I saw beauty in the hills, Truth shone in life's maze.

*Betty Mealand*

**DOWN BY THE MIRY BROOK**

By a secret stile, one Summer eve,
        Down by the Miry Brook,
A Shortwood lad and a Nailsworth girl
        Loitering, lingering took
The furtive fruits of a fond farewell
        And showed with anguished look
How harsh is the hour when love must leave
        The lilt of the Miry Brook.

Oh, the Miry Brook will sing through the night
        Of the many loves it has seen
On its busy journey from Sallywood
        To the millpond's moonlit sheen,
Where Horsley and Avening waters wait
        For tales of the wooded dene,
Whose trees conspire to hide from sight
        Loves that should not be seen.

By a secret stile, one Winter day
        Down by the Miry Brook
The Nailsworth girl in anguish bid
        Its lilting waters look
For her Shortwood lad of summer lost;
        But the speechless stream now took
No heed as it fled to depths far off
        Where mill wheels thundered and shook.

*Bill Reid*

## GENTLE LADIES

There is a ferry at Hampton Loade
Where two sisters find abode.
A bell is rung for them to hear
Short time to wait, they then appear
Down the path from house on high
One at the pole and one to untie.
The raft floats to where we stand
Grey haired, smiling, one lends a hand
To land lubbers, who may feel unsure.
On board we feel the raft unmoor
Float gently, water rippling as we glide
With current and tide to the other side.
But while we sit and have a chat
To helm lady, who in between us sat,
Garden flowers and fruit; toys around
Knitted in Winter whilst housebound,
Marigolds for just 10p.
A doll for a friend and eggs for tea.

*Meg Pybus*




## PEACE

I looked at the snow on Shropshire's hills
T'was pure and virgin white
Forgot my worries and my pills
And sampled its delights.

For here is peace and tranquillity
The grouse wings whirr in flight
Beneath a cloak of driven snow
The scars of man, hidden from sight.

The moorland road meandered
As far as the eye could see
Nothing moved in this frozen place
Except the rabbits, the grouse and me.

The only footsteps, bar my own
Are the rabbits where they have played
As I stood and looked and felt the peace
Very silently I prayed.

I prayed the peace that I now felt
Could be felt throughout the land
I'm no Angel, but I'm certain sure
My God is close at hand!

*E Ozanne*


## TO THE HILLS OF HOME

Are you clothed with broom and gorse's gold
        While hawks hang overhead?
Do the fern's stiff stems rise tightly rolled
        When other growth seems dead?

Do the skylarks quiver from your crest
        Heavenly descants singing?
Does the short grass shiver on your breast
        With grass-hoppers springing,

And the yaffles fly from hawthorn trees
        In undulating flight?
Are the Priory's bells borne with the breeze
        Heard on the Beacon's height?

Before the last flush of foxgloves fall
        And harebells are too few
I will respond to my hills' homecall;
I'm coming home to you.

*Beryl V Pardoe*

## THE NEW GLOUCESTER CITY

Everything's up to date in Gloucester City,
The work is now completed in Bell Walk.
There are Continental Restaurants
American dishes too
We're the most progressive City you ever saw.
Our brand new clock depicts 'The Tailor of Gloucester'
The children love to watch the well known tale.
It really would have pleased 'Old Doctor Foster'
We know he would have come back without fail.

North, South, East and Westgate Streets are pedestrianised.
The new arcades are all the modern trend.
We love to wander through them
And they keep us warm and dry,
But we have to be aware of what we spend.
Kings Walk leads on to Kings Square with its fountains,
With its stepping stones for little paddling feet.
And scattered round about are trees and benches,
Where many a weary shopper finds retreat.

Yes, everything's up to date in Gloucester City
And old ideas have given place to new
Its fun to take a River trip
And look around the Docks
A visit to Gloucester Ski Slope's worth a view.
The cathedral will remain the same forever,
Restitution work won't change its face.
The centre of Divineness and of God's endless love,
Our principal of beauty and of grace.

**Shirley M Watson**

**NEW TOWN BY NIGHT**

Silence throbs down the street
Houses reach around the despair like a wall
Piercing aloud the rampant fall of feet
Tripping down the road to shop lights call

Two urban lamps shining over two miles
All the street rats feed on night
Blank names and details fallen over police files
These disillusioned many have a similar plight.

Angry young men who work in the light
Express their opinions with art
Graffiti and works of philosophy at night
Leap from the vaults of the heart.

Everyone dies around five
Burnt out cars sail down the lane
Sirens hopelessly chase down 'Alders Drive'
Here's a pint of lager for your pain
Everyone cries at ten
For then it's time to go home
The Saturday shops are shut again
There's nowhere left to roam.

*J Mutchell*

## PHARAOH'S LIGHTHOUSE, FLEETWOOD

That stark impostor Pharaoh's lighthouse
A white surprise in chequered stone,
With shuttered eyes and body anchored
To the street below.

A strange intruder facing seaward
From out the thick of Fleetwood town,
Doomed to squat in brooding silence
As the trams go round.

What architect designed you there,
What bumptious bit of planning
Decreed your fate to idle days
Beside the Wyre Channel?

How odd to think you'll never mock
An oceanic rage, or feel the sting
Of brackish spray, or warn a ship
Some Godless day!

*Dot Walmsley*




## RISING SEVERN

Southwards the river flows where Worcester meadows
Lie, rain-lashed, helpless 'gainst its Winter surge,
Lapping wet fingers o'er the sodden landscape
Till 'neath its silent tide their contours merge.

Now the new bridge in slender isolation
Marches, pier-like, across an inland sea
Flowing to meet the light-eclipsing Malverns
As waters flare, then, darkly, cease to be.

Leaden-hued skies, downpouring, unrelenting,
Bury the hills and race across the plain;
Mutely the land accepts its watery burden,
Suffering now what will be Summer's gain.

River bank boundaries have no definition;
Hedges are drowned, treetops stand proud, forlorn;
Patient, the four-eared tower of the Cathedral
Gazes downstream - and sees the land re-born!

*Ivy Lee*


## HEREFORD STATION

Victorian buildings grand and splendid,
Brick and stone all mellow stand,
Evening sunshine, length'ning shadows,
Railway lines laid down in strands.

Pigeons search for scraps and breadcrumbs,
People wait in little groups,
Talking slowly, glance at watches;
Flower basket sadly droops.

Here's the engine coming slowly!
Stops - a giant in the steam,
Hissing grunting, keen to go again,
Busy fireman, keeps it clean.

People slowly carry cases,
Cross the bridge, down steps this side;
Tickets taken - out to taxis,
Porter puts the case inside.

Signal drops and guard is ready
Waves his flag, the engine peeps;
Shush, shush, shush its going now and
Then the station quietly sleeps.

*Terence Hutchins*

## SWINESIDE VALLEY

Who could weave a tapestry so perfect?
Gentle browns, greens and flecks of white.
Three dimensional in form with copse and barren rock
the artist and the poet's sheer delight.

In the foreground I pick out a winding road
it meanders like a snake in twists and turns.
Purple foxgloves spike the air as if to paint
a healthy sheen rests on the rich new ferns.

There appears to be the figure of a man upon a hill
the black and white of sheepdogs, stands out proud,
one is crouching very low awaiting orders
the other in response to whistle loud.

Away from all life's hustle, wars and grief and strife
this magic mix of all things good, slowly comes to life.
I sit and admire the splendour and note in the distance, a cry
a bird of prey is hovering, a tasty morsel caught its eye.

The shepherd on the hillside calls his canine friends
to help him bring the erring sheep back home, around the bends.
A million strands of silver, trek the mountains, cool
tumbling over mossy stones to create a natural pool.

This outstanding beauty, is woven not with threads of gold and green
it is the natural fabric of the earth, intertwined, which forms the scene.
The ultimate of tapestries fashioned by God's own hand
is a tiny taste of Heaven, in the beautiful Lake Land!

*Barbara Eastham*

## ON CENTRAL PIER

On the pier, a pigeon pecked a Smartie
that some little kid had crushed in spite
a tiny smudge of chocolate, its sugar coat an atoll
once lipstick red and kiss me quick,
now pulverised to white.

Almost kicked and put to flight, the pigeon whirled
before a gang of girls, all gel and mousse
with hair, more rats tails piled on top than curls,
there, throwing balls, a pound for two
to try to knock three bottles off
to win an unappealing pig decked out in spotted fur.

And, just for her, a skinny, spotty lad was bouncing
basket balls into a net, or not
to try to win a purple chimpanzee
for her, the little blonde who's wonder-bra
restricted blood flow to his brain.

Above our heads, intended to impress
the flags of Europe raised on poles, had
gunned themselves to powder in a summer-long succession
of strong to gale force westerlies.
Red in shreds, the Tricolour a Deuxcolour
had borne the brunt of most of them it seemed.

The people look so poor, she said, and yet
they act like lemmings just to own an orange crocodile.
It's rather sad, I said, and we agreed and wandered out
beneath the high steel Ferris Wheel
turning slowly overhead. A second's peace,
the perching pigeon saw its chance
and pounced upon the Smartie once again.

*John Tirebuck*

## SOMERSET, SOMERSET

Somerset, Somerset, how pleasant you are
Whether walking or cycling, or driving by car
The sea, though not perfect, most beaches suffice
And your climate though damp, can at times be nice.

Somerset, Somerset your land undulates
No jagged bleak mountains, where the snow line gyrates
Graceful your hills, from Brent Knoll to Brean
And the line of the Mendips with its heathery sheen.

Somerset, Somerset, from your dykes to your dunes
And your characteristic cider based tunes
You exude so much interest, its rich in your pores
Those thatched roofed cottages, with weather-worn doors!

Somerset, Somerset, you're the county of choice
The top of the range, geographic Rolls Royce
From Minehead to Clevedon, or inland to Street
You're scenerys superb and countryside sweet.

Somerset, Somerset, as the sunset fades
And night falls silent in Exmoor's glades
The owl hoots hard, beneath the height
Of a clear as crystal Somerset night.

Somerset, Somerset, from the Severn due South
Delightful, delicious, you water the mouth
Victorian Clevedon and the Crescents of Bath
To fine country inns, logs aglow in the hearth.

Somerset, Somerset, so verdant and fresh
Behold! All your hedgerows a wildflower mesh
I walk through your lanes, and love to roam far
Thinking Somerset, Somerset, how pleasant you are!

*Nicholas Winn*

**THE HAUNTED CHURCH**

St Marys at Avenbury lies in a ruin now
Hidden from the seeing eye
Nature cast her veil, and made a claim
The bell was first to go, removed before the War
Taken up to London Town, so the story's told
To some place called St Andrew by the Wardrobe.
Maybe it hangs there still.

Dark brooding yew trees stand
Pagan sentinels to those who sleep beneath the ground
No flowers placed among the hidden mounds
Yet every Springtime, near the churchyard wall
Snowdrops in profusion bloom,
Petals touched a verdant bright, blending with soft
Moss that grows upon the stone.

The lonely little Church is haunted, some are heard to say
When all was still and empty, sweet organ music plays,
Drifting out along the valley.

Folks who deal with the 'paranormal' came, nothing did they find
St Marys kept her secret, even until this time.
Maybe it is only the murmuring river, flowing on its way
Perhaps the only ghost is the Holy Ghost - who can say?

*A Dolan*

## VIEW FROM PILLING SHORE (PART 2)

So contrastingly stark and dark
Against nature's true beauty reality:
As sandy brown brine bay waters watch
And lap at the feet of Lakeland's Hills' side

Frowning up pale blue distant mounts
Now clouded in shroud
- Are they that mourn mountains or mist?
Yet still do they move!
As ships that steam on towards each other
But in this daytime anyway
They never quite seem to meet!

Thus contemplating, then completing
A whole half new Panorama View
As distant meccano crane gantries
Pointing ever upwards
Collectively spike the sky
So Hail Ho! Barrow
Part submerged in Irish Sea and sky.

Horizon and Outlook have been brighter
Like other specialist marine builder
Work and order books fuller
But unlike that poor old ship
From middle eastern desert
'Lord of Liverpool',
They haven't been completely sunk yet!

So let's try and be thankful to God
For all that we have got.

*Mack A Duerden*

## MY LANCASHIRE

When people think of Lancashire
It brings a picture to mind
Of factory chimneys and coal pits
When there's so much more you'll find.

Rolling hills to climb, covered with heather
A gently breeze caressing your face
See Winters hoar frost, sprinkling the grass
With a sparkling white pattern of lace.

In Springtime, trees burst into bud
As crocus and snowdrops appear
Summer brings a carpet of bluebells
In the wood by a tranquil mere.

Cool treelined roads and avenues
Rivers, canals and streams
Country walks, their picturesque beauty
Fill your wildest dreams.

Stroll leisurely by the canal
As longboats and barges drift past
Long necked swans and ducks aplenty
Why do we live life so fast?

Relax in the cool of the evening
As the sun drops behind the hill
Sated by thoughts of tomorrow
That Lancashire can fulfill.

*Esma Banham*

## OH LANCASHIRE

Oh Lancashire, my Lancashire
Of hot pot, pie and peas
Of Rovers and of North-end
Both scoring goals with ease

Blackpool has its Pleasure Beach
Its golden tower and mile
Morecambe has Frontier land
And Mr Blobby's smile.

The Time Team's been to visit us
To study Roman life
In the very place where I was born
And where I met my wife!

The Lake District's a drive away
It's a very pleasant land
We've sport and art and history
'Cos Lancashire life's real grand!

***David Charnley***


## GLEVUM

Cam Peak, Long Down and Smallpox Hill
Uley Bury, - its earthworks still.

Roman legions marching came,
Left Woodchester a mosaic fame.

Stinchcombe Hill and Berkeley Vale,
The Severn shines a liquid trail.

Cathedrals, Castles, Stately Homes
Hills and Vales wherein to roam.

Villages of golden tone
With Market Halls of Cotswold stone.

Burial mounds upon the hills,
Old woollen towns with watermills

This county hidden in the West
Has secrets still with which its blessed.

For Paradise - well earned its name
And Gloucestershire, one and the same.

*Jean Price*


## LOOKING TOWARDS GLOUCESTER FROM LONGFORD

It's a pleasure to stand at my window and gaze at the scene displayed
I can stand and stare for an hour or more, as I would at a grand parade
For beyond the end of my garden, and over the grassy mound
Lies, not only a busy by-pass, but also a sporting ground
And there standing proud on the sky line, dwarfing the buildings nearby
The magnificent Gloucester Cathedral stretches its spires to the sky.

I can watch on a Summer's morning the stirring of life's busy day
A bird catching worms in the garden, sparse traffic along the highway
There are always some early risers, with their dogs taking them for a run
And often a track suited jogger, all enjoying the morning sun
Then through the hours the scene will change, and maybe I shall view
A football game or a cricket match before the day is through.

With winter nigh, the Plock Court seagulls come back multiplied.
Fog shrouds the road and field beyond, and sounds are magnified.
Then later when the rain brings floods and the grounds are frozen hard
The children sliding on the ice, make a scene for a Christmas Card.
But my favourite view is after dark, as car beams slice the night
And there for all of us to see, the Cathedral bathed in light

*Eleanor West*

## BEHIND THE CANDY FLOSS

Our Weston super Mare resort, beside the Bristol Channel
Calls out for kiddies to bring spades and buckets of enamel
Its miles of silvery-golden sand offers countless pleasures
While at its end, in rock-pool bay, children can search for treasures
The Grand Pier offers its delights, candy-floss, ice-cream, fun rides
The Tropicana lets folk swim, and have lots of fun on slides.
The Arcades sound their noisy tunes, if amusement is desired.
Or Beach Lawns offer quiet rest if you are feeling tired.
The wafting smells of fish and chips tempt many appetites,
But perhaps you'd like to leave all that and see our other sights?
Out of town we have three parks, hilly Ashcombe, Clarence, Grove
Their shady quiet flowered grounds are requesting you to rove
A lovely walk through shaded woods watching the squirrels at play
Or stroll right through to other side and survey Kewstoke Bay.
Out at sea lie two islands, of Steep Holm and of Flat Holm,
And Brean Down juts out from the shore, offering its welcome.
Uphill too, lies at this end with small boats in a harbour
Or you could climb its church-topped hill, if you've an hour or more.
In town we have a good museum, which tell our ancient history
Of Roman finds and skeletons and many an other mystery.
Some miles away lies Cheddar Gorge and Cheddar Caves and Wookey
Where witch is said to sit in stone, it really is quite spooky.
So, branch out from the candy-floss, enjoy our other sights,
There's more to us than Kiss Quick hats and pretty sea-front lights.

*Beryl Kearns*

**THE DELL AT HUNT END**

At the foot of the dell
I glimpsed a black silhouette against the fading sky
An old Willow sitting on his throne.

At the foot of the dell
I listened to the gentle murmur of the wood:
A mirror of my heart.

At the foot of the dell
Twinkled the lights of a distant farm
Reflected in my eyes

At the foot of the dell
The weeping willow had gone
But I finally knew the truth.

*Jamie Lewis*


**SEASON CURLS**

Seaweed high, sand so bare,
Wrap up warm to stand and stare,
Sea of grey, wave curls of cream,
Winter sunlight, dreary scene.

Seaweed swept away,
In the springs of May,
Sea of green, wave curls of grey,
Spring sunlight prepares the way.

Buckets of water, castles of sand,
Deckchair tickets, hear the band,
Sea of blue, wave curls of white,
Summer sun, heart's delight!

*Valerie J Knopp*

## WESTON SUPER MARE

As a seaside resort its popularity started in Victorian times
Brunel's railway opened the way for visitors as well as conveying Bath stone
To build crescents and terraces of large houses, business men commuted by rail.
Local limestone was quarried for detached villas - soon bought by retired people,
Whose wealth enabled them to employ live in servants as little industry here.
Shops lit by gas, closed late, elaborate displays behind plate glass windows.
The bays' views made up for the far receding tide, newly built Birnbeck Pier prospered
People embarked on pleasure boat trips, walked, bathed, rode donkeys, such simple enjoyment
Statutory Holidays meant a large influx of families seeking a change,
Weston needed to enhance its attraction with new ideas and forward planning.

Sand dunes were replaced by lawns, roads, a retaining sea wall and esplanade was built.
Holiday makers lodged in boarding houses, their own food then cooked by the Landladies!
The wide beach was ideal for souvenir and refreshment stalls, Punch and Judy shows,
Animal acts, Pierrots, Minstrels and the Salvation Army daily gathered crowds.
Along the shore line donkeys gave rides, plodding ponies pulled children's high ornate carts
The Grand Pier was built, suffered a fire, and re-opened in nineteen thirty two

This provided a place to stroll, fish, or try amusement machines and the fun fair.
The open air swimming pool on the sea front - its diving board a major feature
Plus a model yacht pond built on the beach and new cinemas in the town
Were novel experiences for the masses arriving from grey suburbia
The Marine Lake was formed by a causeway trapping the sea, a children's paradise
Paid entry gave safe swimming, paddle boats, a water chute, rafts and a youngsters' funfair,
The colonnaded walkway with its canvas changing cubicles in constant use.
World War two bombing led to new industries and estates, giving rise to guest houses.
Annual bathing beauty contests were a regular well attended event.
Latterly Birnbeck Pier is in disarray, the Grand Pier amusements updated.
No marine Lake attractions I enjoyed as a child, the floral clock still delights.
Shopping malls, supermarkets jostle for space near the most wonderful museum.
Many West Country adults have fond memories of Sunday School outings with friends.
A new Pier and Sea Life Centre the latest addition to its bracing sea front.

*M E Beale*

## AVALON

Mystic isle, rising from Sedgemoor Vale,
legend of Joseph and the Holy Grail.
Glastonbury, Isle of Avalon so dear,
were Arthur and Guinevere buried here.
Ancient thorn that on Wearyall stands,
did Joseph once hold you in his hands.
Your blossoms at Christmas still to be found
upon the hill and hallowed ground.
Is it fable, is it myth, or more,
did he land on your swampy shore,
plant his staff and watch it grow,
build that first chapel long ago.
St Michael's tower on your heights
some say on ancient leyline sights.
Earth's energy, mysteriously arranged in lines,
elemental rods deflect, perceive the signs.
Linking sacred sites where worship was held,
from whence these unknown forces welled.
As you quietly enter the ambience enthrals,
peace and tranquillity within your walls.
Chalice well, spring so pure, of Christ bled,
Iron reddens your shimmering stream's bed.
Soak up the water's flowing sounds,
was the Holy Grail hidden in your grounds.
Glastonbury, thoughts of you drive this pen,
why are we drawn to you, time and again.
Such haunting beauty and atmosphere lures,
Avalon, your myth and legend still endures.

*Bob Woodroofe*

## GLOUCESTERSHIRE CHURCHES

Churches abound in Gloucestershire County
Wool from the sheep was a wonderful bounty.
Some Churches are large and the houses are few
Who goes to Church now, or fills up a pew?
Each Church is unique and a joy to behold
The walls are thick stone that keep in the cold.
Spires and turrets and towers for a bell
And are we for heaven, or are we for hell?
Who drew the plans and who paid the money?
Whose ancestors hewed stone the colour of honey?
Find some wall paintings, rare in the land,
See the niche outside, where the leper could stand.
The churchyards are full and the tombstones are slanted,
Here and there fresh flowers have been planted.
The skull and the crossbones denote the plague years
Those bones won't be dug up - have no fears!
Go inside and feel the prayers and the love
Gaze at the roof, like a boat, high above.
Wonder who polishes the brass till it glows
Sweeps between the seats kept mostly in rows;
Whose hands tend the flowers, keep clean the altar cloth,
Mends the roof, mows the grass, dusts away spider and moth?
Keeps the Church clean for the day of the bride
Waits to comfort families of those who have died,
Tends the font for the babes to be brought
And waits for the Christian Church to be sought.
The Cotswold Churches have stood there for years
Watched joy and laughter, pain and tears.
Neglect these buildings and how sad it would be,
If there were no more Gloucestershire Churches for you and for me.

*Diana Maslen*

## BRONZE AGE BOAT

People clutching at the wire,
Peering into the time tunnel
In the chasm beneath the tarmac.
A mummified boat -
Preserved in the black ooze
Of the esturine mud.

Three thousand years ago
The boat foundered;
Jettisoned its cargo of bronze
And limped into the shelter
Of the harbour -
Settling into oblivion.

Thick planks, hewn by men
To fit together and held
By pegs and brackets;
Twine, binding pieces
Through millennium - holding
Past and present.

Removed from its urban grave;
Freed of its shroud of slime;
It will be pieced together, pumped full
Of new life - kept for all to ponder.
A resurrection!
The Dover Bronze Age boat!

*Edwina Gray*

## THE VIEW FROM MY WINDOW

At night I look from my window
And there is darkness like black velvet
Then beyond, lights like jewels
Strung out, scattered and strewn
Stretching far into the distance
Flickering and glittering until
There is blackness again
And that is the Sea.

On clear days I look from my window
And the world spreads out before me
There are cows in a field and sometimes sheep
There is a windmill, clean and white but
With only one sail. There are hills and woods
And across the rooftops of the town
Sparkling in the distance
I can see the Sea.

When I look from my hilltop window
I survey the world from on high like God
But when the mists roll in from the sea
The hills and woods, the fields and rooftops
Disappear, hidden under its swirling grey fingers
The sea is a secret lost from sight
The lights are dimmed and I am, after all
Only mortal.

*Anne Dearle*

## ON ROUTE A29

We start our journey south to Bognor Regis by the Sea
On Route A29, which begins near Beare Green actually

Passing Ockley, Slimfold and Five Oakes on through
To 'Sotheby's, at Summers Place, could peruse, purchase an antique or two!

Linger awhile in Billinghurst, glimpse the local fare
Take a peep inside my old home, shall I knock the door, do I dare?

Remembering in 1963, fields and farmland my dog and I once strolled
Now house Light Industry and Residential Estates untold.

The High Street saw much traffic even then, with such a band
Of excited Day Trippers in Red Double Deckers, enroute for sea and sand

Coaches, carrying punters headed for the Glorious Goodwood Course
Hoping to turn their bets into winnings, via a cert' Racehorse!

The village once swarmed with Actors, Technicians and a whole Company
For the filming of 'Ever Decreasing Circles', later to be seen on TV

Other notables have graced the area, like Diana Dors, and many more
On the commuter belt it lies, accessible for those to London, working
9 to 4.

Moving on to Pulborough, where the River Arun, floods each year
On lower pastures green, Watersfield is aptly named, water-birds
flock here.

The climb up Bury Hill, gradient of about 1 in 7, reveals an unbeatable
view
Naturally wonderful, many times captured on canvas, hopefully that's
true.

If car makes it to the top!, park at Whiteways, take a beechwood walk
Before detouring slightly down the B2139 to the Museum of Amberley
Chalk.

Browse at machinery, plus implements - used on the land in times of old
Then sit beside the busy River Arun, where 'naughty but nice' teas
are sold!

I will give Arundel a miss, 'cos it would take all my time to seek
Its history, within the castle walls alone, could take another week.

So down to Fontwell, head straight on for the South Coast - passing by
Bersted North and South, Hooray - at Bognor Regis, the sea I finally spy!

*A Richards*


## CUCKMERE

Shaft of sunlight on the water
Green, then grey and running free
Nature sends her lovely daughter
Cuckmere River to the sea.

On and on, she twists and turns
Each bend she knows, will lead her home
Home to join the never ending sea
Of rushing foam.

Waves run up to serenade her
Making music, as they rise
Foamy patterns showing off their beauty
To the skies.

Ebbing tide joins in the dance
The lullaby she sings is sweet
Moonlight sees her jig and prance
Her journey is complete.

*P Byers*

## AVON RADIO REPORT

It was reported that she'd often been seen there
Sitting, staring waiting to care?
Indeed in the hope he'd return.

As the University Tower chimed ten
They would meet, embrace.
Furtive glances as they hurried to their den.
That night he was uncommonly late.
Something was wrong, her perception correct
'This is where it ends, it must'.
Silencing her soft whimpered protest
By one last kiss.

Still she would go and wait, pretend,
Imagine their meetings as
Owners called back their four-legged best friends
Disapproving of the lone woman
Possible danger - inevitable.

Found strangled on the Downs
The radio bleated as he ate
Not his fault, he'd told her weeks before
Yet knowing she was there to wait
Guilt washed over him.

It was reported that she'd often been seen there
'It was bound to happen, perhaps she wanted it
Eat your toast dear'.

He returned to his breakfast - his wife to the sink
Deserved it? Asked for it? No, not that.

But she would pester him so
What else was he to do?

Still he cried as he jumped.
'Clifton Suspension Bridge, famed for suicide...'

**Judith Corrigan**

**COME AND SEE**

The attractions here are endless
There's things to do and see
Some you have to pay for
But many of them are free.

At Margate there is Dreamland
An enjoyable place for all
Across the road the golden sands
And the enticing waves that call.

Now Ramsgate is a wonderful sight
There's the beach and the West Cliff too
The glorious views and endless walks
There's loads there for you to do.

Broadstairs is a quaint old town
It's an interesting place to be
The traditional pubs and coffee bars
There's so many things to see.

You can venture out on country walks
And visit country pubs
Or you can find the night life
In our popular and friendly clubs.

In Thanet you will always find
Heaps of things to do
There will always be an attraction
That will bring enjoyment to you.

*Jacqui Pittock*

## KENT'S RIVER

Born in Sussex, to Penhurst the muddy Medway flows
where it with Eden intertwines and
man has built a dam to tame the river's flow.
Soon it parts to surround a well-kept pleasure ground
to wind its way past Norman castle keep,
leaving Tonbridge by flat green and golden land
to meet the Beult and Teise, at times to flood.
Yalding and the Lees.
Over weirs and under ancient bridges run
to pools where snow white water lily grow,
a place for dragon-flies to drone.
Past oast and farm, to wooded primrose slopes.
Then onto Maidstone town, capital of Kent.
Shortly Medway meets the tide
and turns to silver on mixing with the sea.

*Michael J Hills*


## SOUNDS OF HARMONY

Beautiful sounds I hear through my wall
Melodious music to my ear
Morris Dancer and singer too
Practising their artistry near.

Over the weekend just gone by
The Morris Dancers jingled
Beautiful bells as they pranced around
Leaving the people to mingle.

Hastings Town on Bank Holiday
Reminded me of times gone by
Jollity and crowded streets
Under the blue, blue sky.

*Mary West*

## OLD MOTHER GORING

The byways of Sussex were rich in folklore,
And Wiston and Washington had their own store;
They said, when the Weather Clerk went to his tap,
'Old Mother Goring is wearing her cap!'

Now, Washington geese own a very small brook,
In midsummer drought for a shower they look;
So, gazing up eastwards, their wings they will clap
If Old Mother Goring is wearing her cap!

A bushy green tonsure had crowned her with grace;
Along the escarpment she held pride of place;
But hurricane winds have torn many a gap,
So. . . Old Mother Goring is wearing a cap!

A lady who lived at the foot of the hill
(And for all that I know she is living there still)
Would sit by the fireside, her cat in her lap,
When Old Mother Goring was wearing her cap.

The Great House at Wiston's a fine sight to see,
With a subway for toads to a lake on the lea -
But when you go walking, take brolly and wrap,
If Old Mother Goring is wearing her cap!

*Joyce Birchall*

## FROM HOME ... BY TRAIN

As quickly as the train takes me away
From the protective shade of the oak
So the clouds meander across the sky
Blossoms and branches travel past me
Or do I them?

Ewes with their young quietly
Meditating people as they devour the grass
Cautiously.

Apple orchards, buds and leaves anew
Prepare to yield Kent's finest fruit
Sunshine yellow mustard
Sparkling in the distance.

Grassy fields torn apart by turfers
Hop poles naked line the farmland.

The Kentish oast weather vane
Points from my sanctuary
And yet I never leave this place
Though my body may travel afar
Part of me is always here.

*Moreen Smythe*

**SOUTH EASTERN ENGLAND**

To live in the South East of England
May not be everyone's dream
But I'm sure, when the world was created
It formed part of His wondrous scheme.

Its villages, quaint and old fashioned
Worth more than a cursory look
For you'll find, if you delve into history
Their names in the Doomsday Book.

Its Cities, Cathedral spires towering
Over castles, walls crumbling with age.
Their names made immortal by Dickens
In his books that we've read, page by page.

Just visit the marshes at Romney
Now home for the hundreds of sheep
Once favourite haunt of the smugglers
Who came while the town was asleep.

Garrison towns, full of soldiers and sailors
Cinque Ports to keep enemies in sight
Its Dockyards - ships in for a re-fit
Repaired, once more ready to fight.

In war-time this corner of England
Took easily more than its share
Of the terror that swept across Europe
With the bombs raining down from the air.

And 'treasures' you'll find in the South East
Not merely the financial kind
In Spring, orchards laden with blossom
With Summer's hot days close behind
In Autumn its golden days shorten
Then Winter's first snowfall we'll find.

*S Knowles*

**KENT**

By shingle banks surrounded deep
foaming tides of Orchards cling
like dreams - a countryside asleep
each dewdrop morning sparkling.

Returned again the Summer skies
hayfield scents the land full-spent
with hop and apple Cornflower blaze
rewrites old tales of native Kent.

Frosty-fretted cobwebs spring
on tethered Oasts - Hop poles peep
through ancient hedges.  Thrushes wing
o'er scattered farms and rice-grain sheep.

Autumn fogs, tests to the wise-
ethereal landscapes, napkin white
'neath Winter snows in Ermine guise
and evenings don the Cape of night.

*V Weston*

**DEAR DOVER**

I moved away for several years,
But found it hard to stem the tears
That flowed upon my pillow white,
That eased my yearning through the night.

My dreams were nearly all of home,
The place that I had left to roam
To see the world and all its sights.
To taste the wonder and delights.

But now my wandering days are over,
And I am back in my dear Dover,
The place where I was born. You see,
There's nowhere else on earth for me.

My roots are deep, my love too strong
To stay away for very long.
This place with castle, cliffs and sea
Is the very world to me.

*Winnie May*


## OUR PARK

In May red chestnut blossoms drift down
On the paths where the womenfolk walk into town,
And in summer long evenings resound to the shout
Of *howzat* as their best all-rounder is out.
As the white clad figures meet in their game
Like their grandfathers did in this park just the same.

The little ones laugh as they tumble around
A-swinging high in their own hallowed ground
And away in a corner the pleasing ping
Of a well placed service as ball meets string.

So busy this park yet so quiet withal
Green and serene and away from it all.
While the church stands aloof but with kindly eye
Chimes the happiest hours as days go by
With a great peal of bells just to say all is right
When the bell ringers practise on Monday night.

*Monica F Leppard*

## FROM A STILE IN KENT (1981)

The air is refined
yet the birds bravely chirrup
but you just can't get away
from the technological din;
England is too small for it
What the hells gone right with the world we're in?

This scarred and scourged land
has been made a new race track
a permanent Brand's Hatch, Biggin Hill
or railroad show that will never be ended.
Blind progress must be stopped if this world's to be saved!

Rot, Roar, Pylons, Pylons
Corrugated iron, corroded Barbed Wire
Rusty nails, rusty pylons, fume, fume, Quake, Bang!
Houses protruding, tasteless, ugly, man-made.
But the bird sings, chirps aloud - a reminder of hope?
Sticky tarmac, Tarmac, stink!

Stop, stop: everyone rest a while,
the course can be altered,
If only a little sense will prevail.
Stop, look, listen! See how we've gone wrong
Use our brains to help - not hinder!

Clamped in your safety belts of secured order
Loosen your collars and look.
Be brave to sing as you want,
The birds have done better than us!

*M J Timms*

## THE JOY OF THE GARDEN OF ENGLAND

The world is wide and varied
Some lands are hot or cold
But Kent is The Garden of England
A joy for all to behold.

Some lands have mountains or chasms
Their landscapes are new or old
But Kent is The Garden of England
A joy for all to behold.

Others have tropical forests
Or lakes and fiords untold
But Kent is The Garden of England
A joy for all to behold.

To hear skylarks over our Downland
Or see foxes and badgers so bold
Oh, Kent is The Garden of England
A joy for all to behold.

The apple blossom in Springtime
Or the Autumn leaves that are gold
Oh, give me The Garden of England
A joy for me to behold!

***Geoffrey J Martin***

## HERE IN KENT

Hey you with the hair
Are you going to the fair
Down the winding Country Lane
It's in the fields.

Oh, look there's the Sea
Yes this is the life for me
Oh what more could someone need
It's here in Kent.

Mmm, smell that rose
The perfume drifting up my nose
In a Garden full of beauty
Here in Kent

Don't walk away
We have so much to see today
Historic Buildings on our way
Here in Kent.

Oh, beg my pardon
For not mentioning the Hop Gardens
Here in Kent.

Don't walk away
We've only just began the day
And over there you see the Farmer
Reaping tons of bales of hay.

Hey you with the hair
Get a ticket for the train
When you've seen the South East's beauty
You'll always want to come again.

***Sheralyn Kent***

**BEXLEYHEATH BROADWAY**

Our Broadway's been pedestrianised
A joy for all to share
But, isn't it a pity
There are those who do not care?

There are litter bins provided
To keep the paved way neat
But paper still adorns the road
Aren't there always ones who'll cheat?

A fountain played its silvery jets
Of water in the air
But now its beauty has been spoilt
By those who could not care.

They've filled it up with bubble bath
Coke tins and paper too
The majority are not to blame
It only takes a few.

It only takes a few to spoil
What others should enjoy
On the spot fines for litter louts
Should be our policemen's ploy!.

*Maggie Sparvell*

## MARGATE

Margate is a tired town
Old in years and spirit
But those who deem
To stay each year
Are always sad to leave it.

Though it is an old town
Its memories are clear as day
Of every person past and present
Who came and wished to stay

No grander lady will you find
Full of hope and pride
For along every golden sand
Is the ever changing tide.

Her voice has slowly changed
From the years afar
From the clarity of the horse and cart
To the muffled roar of the car

But although she is old
Her time is not yet done
So come to dear old Margate
And bask in her welcoming sun.

*Kate Beerling*

## THE COUNTIES OF KENT AND EAST SUSSEX

There's a garden in Kent where the flowers are gay,
      And the apple trees bloom in the spring,
Where the blackbird sings on the orchard bough,
      What a beautiful song he sings.

The River Medway flows gently by,
      Where the Friary of Aylesford stands,
And the Carmelite monks there work and pray,
      With their rosaries held in their hands.

A beautiful garden it is indeed,
      Where gaily the flowers grow in spring,
The bluebells nod in the woodland glade,
      And what great joy they bring.

The hop fields of Kent are there to behold,
      And the skylark sings high above,
Where the fleecy clouds float gently by,
      It is indeed a song of love.

In Sussex the Downs roll down to the sea,
      And the tall white cliffs can be seen,
So when the spring time comes again,
      Come down to this land so green.

*Isabella M Collier*

## PLACE NAMES

The Saxon past of Sussex lies hid in many a name
Which tells of folk who lived and died before the Normans came.
They sailed the sea, and claimed the land, and built their homesteads here,
Where names which end in -ing and -ham still keep the record clear.

When storks still came to Storrington, and seals on Selsey lazed,
And crows cawed loud in Crawley, their goats at Gatwick grazed.
Their cows drank deep at Keymer; at Horsham horses neighed,
And coughs were cured with horehound plucked in Arundel's green glade.

And first among their chieftains was Cissa, Aelle's son,
Whose sword made Sussex Saxon, and forced the 'Welsh' to run.
Both Roman camp and iron-age fort bold Cissa's prize became,
And Chichester and Cissbury Ring still witness to his fame.

And others, less illustrious, whose deeds are past recall,
Left names upon our Sussex map familiar to us all:
There's Rusta, Wurth, and Angemaer, to mention but a few,
And Bognor's Lady Bucge, and Goodwood's Godgifu.

Though William came to Pefen's stream, and fought on Haesta's ground,
In this our fair South-Saxon land, few Norman names are found.
Though former farms be villages, and hamlets bustling towns,
Still Saxon names their story tell across the Weald and Downs.

*Mercia MacDermott*

## CHICHESTER YACHT BASIN - A FANTASY

She was beautiful to see
In the fading winter day,
Her bows were broad and handsome
And her sails were bright and gay.

The sun was gently sinking
And the wind was rising slow,
When a sudden impulse stirred me
To a venture down below.

Steps leading to the galley
Were topped with shining brass,
The handrail was of polished oak.
She was a bonny lass.

Before I turned to leave her,
My mind confused with schemes,
To own this buoyant beauty,
I glanced upwards to her beams.

Almost hidden by the shadows,
On a tiny metal plaque,
'Queen of my Dreams' was written,
'This boat belongs to Jack'.

Then I knew my dreams were futile,
I could not own this yacht,
She was someone else's dream boat,
So I left, and soon forgot.

*Flora Groves*

## YOU KNOW YOU'RE IN YORKSHIRE WHEN...

You know you're in Yorkshire when
you have walked for miles and then
Moors lined with heather stretch far and wide
and the beauty and splendour cannot be denied
Dry stone walls in fields of green
with grazing sheep, complete this scene
You pause to look at the spectacular view
and the locals stop and say 'Hello' to you

When you stop at a pub and go in for a bite
the plate is so full and try as you might
you can't eat it all and you feel such a pig
these Yorkshire puddings are just so big!
Villages nestle in the beautiful Dales
like pictures in books of fairy tales
Everyone here seems happy, somehow
that's because, you're in Yorkshire now!

*Irene Taylor*

## CANTERBURY

The many sights that I have seen,
In England far and near.
The ones of Canterbury will always mean,
So very much to me.

The Cathedral majestically rises towards the sky,
With beauty and heritage in every part.
That you will cherish until the day you die,
And will always hold within your heart.

The stained glass windows that make you stare,
As they shine and sparkle in the sun.
Which holds your interest that you'll want to share,
When you see the beauty in everyone.

Our Kentish countryside delights,
Or the Garden of England as it's known.
Intrigues the tourists with its many sights,
And reigns supreme upon England's throne.

*Roy R Hackers*


**NOSTALGIC WISTFULNESS**

Soft rolling hills and chalk cliffs steep.
Gold swaying corn, in summer to reap.
Quaint hamlets nestling in valleys deep
with smoke ascending as a dream from sleep.

Children happy on beaches - but sometimes wailing.
Farmers mending their fences - busily nailing.
Ferries packed with cars from Seaports a-sailing,
people lining the deck-rails shouting and hailing.

The watery Flats of the old Romney marshes.
Ancient cathedrals with towering arches
beautifully framed through green swaying larches.
The Royal Marines' bands heading numerous marches.

Sheep flocks meandering with no obvious intent.
Seagulls swooping on scavenging bent.
Cows following leaders as to milking they went.
Acres of fruit trees with blossoming scent.
This is *my* home . . . this County of Kent.

*J Bryant*

## SEVEN SISTERS

Seven Brides for Seven Brothers
Is a worldwide famous show,
But who seeks the Seven Sisters
To East Sussex fain must go.

Arm in arm, with chalk-white faces,
They stand guard upon the shore,
Never flinching from their places
Despite the ocean's roar.

Where meanders of the Cuckmere
Wind their way towards the sea,
You'll find Cliff End (or Haven Brow) -
A proud first Sister she.

Short Brow keeps watch beside her,
With Rough Brow close at hand,
Brass Point then marks the Crowlink Gap,
Once famed for contraband.

Next Flagstaff Point flanks Bailey's Hill
And last a hill called Went
(Some claim another unnamed hill
The number should augment).

Beyond, you come to Birling Gap,
No Sister stands guard here,
And so erosion takes its toll
Relentlessly each year!

*Aubrey M Woolman*

**KENT**

So this is Kent, old England's garden fair,
With chalky cliffs containing fossils rare,
With sandy bays where it is safe to play,
Where urban children picnic for a day.
While ruined Churches of their past stay mute,
When cobbles rang with sound of smuggler's boot.
And rolling orchards dressed with blossoms white,
Hear sound of foxes calling in the night.
The dykes, where graceful herons stand and stare,
And long-legged lambs can gambol everywhere.
When rushing winds bring fury, noise, and fright,
How nice to snuggle warm in bed at night.
Where sunsets look like master-painted art,
And yet to copy - one could never start.
What tales the men of Kent can often spin,
To fire the mind, for memories to begin.
Though ugly motorways your face may mar,
You find Kent's heart before you journey far.
And this is Kent, so varied and so green,
Please never change, for much to most you mean.

*B Hussey*


**LEGANANNY**

O gentle slopes, witness to countless ages
Bridled by rugged steps and sharpened scales
Winter snow casts a mantle o'er thy brow
Warm summer breezes kiss and tease thy grassy vales

How brave were they that dwelt amongst your portals
In ancient times in hovels formed with stone
Hewn from thy face immortal, now unchanging
And set upon thy brindled fissured throne

*William Dunlop*

## SOUTHERN VIEWS

It is a privilege to live in this beautiful part of the land
And if you came to visit you would soon understand
With cathedrals and churches that are so very old
Also modern architecture which is majestically bold
It is steeped in culture and full of dark mystery
There are rambling hills and forests kissed by the sea
Flowers and colour cover the fields and the dales
Yachts speeding along with billowing sails
The old village green of which the proud villagers boast
It's the oldest and prettiest on the south coast
With old customs and crafts and modern industry
Gable houses, pubs and the delights of a cream tea
Old yokels and the gentry who take their horses out to ride
Lively entrepreneurs all of whom live amicably side by side
This part of the land is so modern but has interesting history
Is why we are so proud to live in the south of this country.

*David Jenkins*


## CONTRASTING ESSEX

*Essex is a county of contrasts*

Of thatched cottages and tower blocks
Housing estates and hamlets.

*A county of colours*

Yellow rape fields and red, white and blue Tube trains
Silver rail track and brown bridle path.

*It is a county of shapes*

Of white-sailed old windmills and snaking new motorway
Factory chimneys and grey church spires.

*It is a county*
Of Docks, rivers and coast
Of farms, industrial estates and village greens

Aerodrome, leisure complex and country pub abound
All this, and more, can be found
*In Essex.*

***J Little***


## BEACHY HEAD

Down in the valley the wind may be quiet and gentle all the day long,
But on Beachy Head it can gust to a galeforce, frighteningly cold
                                                        and strong;
Seahorses ride on the ocean, the clouds rush across the sky,
While the seagulls, soaring, diving, blown by the wind go by.
Massive and high, the great chalk cliffs tower above the sea;
Laced with flint and white and shining, precipitous rock and scree
Descend by more than five hundred feet to the shingle far below,
Where the seabirds, sailing, gliding, alone may safely go.

The wind on the summit of Beachy Head ripples the short-cropped grass,
The birds blow sideways, beating the air and flapping their wings
                                                        as they pass;
Far, far below is the lighthouse: like a tiny toy it stands,
But in stormy weather, shielding, guarding, it saves ships from many lands.
The winds that are strong on Beachy Head can fill the mind with fear;
Down in the valley is greater safety, for perils are always here,
Yet within sight in the fields, quietly there, where the Downs rise
                                                        to meet the sky,
The sheep are grazing, resting and the wind seems to pass them by.

***M E Lang***

## CHRISTMAS PRESENTS - TRYING OUT BIKES
*(Experimental cycle lane - Worthing promenade)*

From seas seen hazily beyond the beach
A damp mist crept across the promenade;
Bikes wobbling crazily, just out of reach,
Two screaming children pedalled past us hard,
Side by side, with great agility,
But well within the newly painted lines,
Breaking in on our tranquillity.
My head chock full of punishments and fines

I saw the shelter looming up ahead;
The cycle lane curved gracefully out and round.
They sped on helter skelter as I said
'Hmph, bloody stupid kids, they're bound
To take a short cut to the other side
And frighten that old lady on the seat'
But no, my expectations were denied;
Tucked one behind the other, nice and neat,

They bombed out breezily around the bend,
Still sticking strictly to the cycle track;
We watched uneasily right to the end
Where, turning round, they hurtled past us, back
Towards the shelter we had left behind.
'No don't look back' I said, 'We'd better not.'
They may have failed the test (it crossed my mind)
But look what happened to the wife of Lot;

What good, with all that salt out there at sea,
Would pillars of it on the sea front be?

*Patrick Taylor*

## CURRAN ROAD (LIVELY FOLK!)

The harbour town lies quietly sleeping,
First rays of daylight shyly peeping.
The lonely ferry's homeward bound,
To the warning tune of foghorn sound.

Our world's awakened, people bustling,
Here and there, a schoolchild jostling
Ambitious traders blinds unfold,
Their day is made, last items sold!

Cafés list Gourmets Delight,
Time to stop here for a bite.
Friends can't meet you for a cuppa,
Who knows, perhaps they'll have some supper.

Parks are busy, sooner or later,
A young mum wheels perambulator.
Along promenade, teenagers venture,
To visit the local leisure centre.

Cinema bright, the queue is mounting,
Basic Instinct, 'Three coins in a fountain
A drink or two now, at the Bailie,
Or join Dan Campbell's, for a Ceili.

Night has fallen, folk are weary,
Spirits flagging, eyes are bleary.
The church clock chimes, time out of number,
As Curran Road rests in silent slumber.

*Rita O'Rourke*

## DOWN TOWNS ANTIQUES

I have been around the world
And there's no place like home
Dear old County Down
Now that there's me home

I have been around the world
And a collector of antiques I want to be
Come on down to County Down
That's where antiques be found

If you go down today
You'll be in for a big surprise
You'll want to browse and stay all day
In the towns of County Down

There's Grays Hill in Bangor now that there's me part of town
There's quaint and jam packed shops there to be found
There's Comber, Saintfield and Rostrevor
And take the ferry to Portaferry

And don't forget Greyabbey
For all it's little size
Has more antiques shops
Than all the emerald Isle

I've been around the world
And there's no place like home
Dear old County Down
Now that there's me home

*Carson Scott*

COMMUNICATING ACROSS THE BARRIERS

# POETRY NOW REGIONAL
# 1996
# ANTHOLOGIES

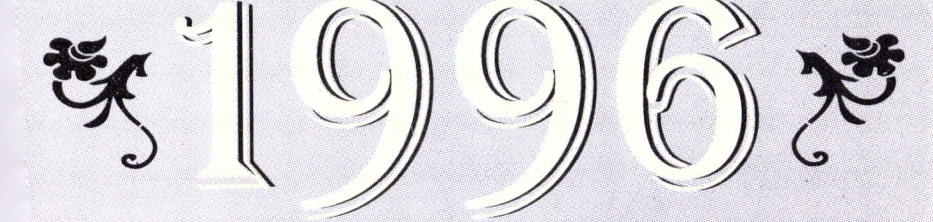

FORERUNNERS IN CREATIVITY AND INSPIRATION.

EDITED BY KERRIE PATEMAN

# POETRY NOW 1996 ANTHOLOGIES

## Order Form

Please supply ___ copy/copies of **Poetry Now Regional Anthology 1996** at £11.99.

I enclose cheque/P.O. for £_____ (Please make cheques payable to Forward Press Ltd.)

**Or**

Please debit my Visa/MasterCard/American Express

Name on Card _____

Card Number _____

Batch Number _____ (American Express only)

Expiry Date _____

Title _____ First Name _____

Surname _____

Address _____

County _____ Postcode _____

Send to:
Poetry Now, 1-2 Wainman Road, Woodston, Peterborough PE2 7BU
Tel: (01733) 230746  Fax: (01733) 230751

*Communicating Across the Barriers*

Code 2

## THE OLD SWINGING BRIDGE

Oh! It's many a night
When the moon it shines bright
And all seems so silent and still
I meet my Colleen
And we walk from the green
Towards the old swinging bridge
    by the mill
Where trees dressed in green
Stand out like a dream
While the moon rises over the hill
We can watch in the west
The sun going to rest
From the old swinging bridge
    by the mill
With the sun going down
And the lights from the town
Casting a glow over old Bernie Hill
My Colleen and I
Watch the years passing by
From the old swinging bridge
    by the mill
Where fishermen stroll
In the cool evening air
With nets that they hope than can fill
And the old 'salmon leap' is a challenge to all
Near the old swinging bridge
    by the mill
It was here Mum and Dad were so happy and glad
When the loom and the plough they were still
With the same moon above they whispered sweet love
On the old swinging bridge
    by the mill.

*Tom McTaggart*

## A DORSET ROMAN ROAD

Down to the Ford where small fishes
        still swim,
there the Roman road climbs to the
        very rim
of the far hill.

Cow Parsley marks the whole width with
        white froth
travelling as did the soldiers of
        Rome's wrath,
against the Britons.

Small flowers fill the rutted road,
        blue Harebell
and the circles of small but bold
        gold Tormentil,
hidden in grasses.

Chalk dust blows, the heat shimmers the
        road ahead,
imagination sees soldiers
        being led
by plumed officers.

Pillage will not be a planned part
        of our day;
we are here to enjoy on this
        old roadway -
Only the wild flowers.

*Mary S Evans*

**BENEATH THE SOUTHERN SUN**

I'm sitting quietly in my chair
And thinking about the passing years.
Where I've been - what I've done
Living beneath the Southern sun.

I think of the journeys
Through green countryside.
The people I've met
Who smile with their eyes.

The hills I have climbed,
The magnificent views,
Showing the beauty
The South offers you.

I think of the streets
That I've walked along,
Sharing the thrill
Of a bustling throng.

I think of the visits
To old seaside towns.
Walking the beaches
With waves lapping round.

I think of the blessings
That I have received
In the South part of England
And give thanks constantly.

*June Rampton*

## BEER: A DEVON VILLAGE

In the cliff's elbow, safe and sound,
Close to the sea, where many drowned
In days gone by, the village lies
Linked to the past with lasting ties.

A babbling brook runs by the road.
In rain-storms, when it overflowed,
It drenched pavements with mud and loam
And the cottages built of stone.

The chalky cliff face bites the sea;
White teeth wrenched huge rock boulders free,
Dashed them with force into the spray,
Torn from their roots on stormy day.

The sea flings pebbles at the beach
Then sucks them back, lest out of reach
They choose to rest and want to stay
Far out of their tormentor's way.

Stranded like whales, the fishing boats
Lie beached with lobster pots and floats,
Waiting 'til they are put to sea
In search of fresh mackerel for tea.

Through the quirky quarry caves
The rumbling roar of restless waves
Recalls the smugglers' daring deeds;
Escape routes now concealed by weeds.

Regatta Week: the tourists come
To watch the barrel-rolling won.
But out of season, beauty thrives
And residents enjoy their lives.

*Nicky Dicken-Fuller*

**POOLE**

Poole is a place of adventure!
With history from the past;
Pirates and smugglers are seen here!
When collecting boxes are bashed.

Look out for the tallships, and speedboats!
Some trips may be had in a day!
But the Barfleur to France is magic!
Yes! In its own sort of way!

Trees and flowers in the country!
With birds of a kind in the air!
But the beauty of the wildlife;
There's nothing can compare!

Horses and deer in the forest;
When spring comes round again;
The rhododendron blooming, along
those country lanes!

Corfe Castle in the distance;
Towering in the sky, has an air
of mystery, its secrets!
You may, want to pry!

There are poets past and present,
who write about its wealth!
But Dorset is a beautiful place!
It's good! For your health!

*E Sharpley*

## MY EL DORADO

I long for my own native Ulster,
I pine for its forests so green,
I've travelled the wide world all over,
But nothing can equal the scene
Of the beauty of all of its landscapes
Be it mountain or river or glen,
Someday I'll return to my homeland,
Never to leave it again.

I see in my dreams the lush pastures
Where the cattle contentedly laze,
And the gorse covered hills of the Sperrins
Where the sheep and the reindeer graze,
Then looking beyond to the valley
What a wondrous sight to behold,
For there in the hill sheltered lowlands
The barley is turning to gold.

The charm of the lakes of *Fermanagh*
Filled with brown speckled trout and with bream,
Surrounded by peace and tranquillity
It is every fisherman's dream.
The high lofty mountains of Mourne
They really sweep down to the sea,
And the misty blue hills of Antrim
They daily are calling to me.

Oh yes I'll return to my homeland
When I've finished my working life's toil,
Then when my Creator He calls me
My body will rest in its soil.

**Ena Wilson**

## THE IMMIGRANT'S DREAM

I'm going back to Ireland, where the grass is ever green,
To the land of turf and praties, and daisies by the stream.
Where County Antrim folk are kind and always quick to say,
'Come in, sit down, I'm glad you're here, I'll make a cup of tae.'

They'll give you fresh baked soda spread with home-made jam,
And all the fadge that you could eat and Ballymena ham.
For there's no place else that can compare with their hospitality,
That's why I know I must go back, it's the only place for me.

I want to stroll down Antrim's glens and up Ahoghill Street,
Then out through Cullybackey where the men are digging peat.
I want to see the river Bann as it flows through Portglenone.
Oh yes, I want to go back there, oh yes, I'm going home.

*Betty Hueston*

## DEADMAN'S LANE

'Pon yon' cold and misty hill,
there stands a gallows, tall and still,
the icy wind doth howl all around,
swirling snow silently engulfs the ground.

The tattered noose that swings in the breeze,
has given its victims such little ease,
Oh, blackened gallows there, 'pon the mound,
you haunt each night with eery creaking sounds.

Nearby, a gibbet hangs menacingly, down a lane,
therein doth lie a murderer's mouldering remains,
He once took a knife from inside his coat,
and ran the cold steel blade 'cross a traveller's throat.

All who dare tread this darkened lane beware,
of ghosts and demons and phantoms there,
turn back, because this morbid tale is true,
these spectres and ghouls will be waiting for you!

*David Brasier*

## AMBASSADORS IN RED AND BLUE

Here's to you the Red and Blue
You are our Mersey Pride
Ambassadors of our great game here on Merseyside

There's nothing more you can achieve
In Britain's greatest game
You've shown the world the way to play and sportsmanship's your name

The best to you the Red and Blue
In all you proudly do
For millions, not just thousands are cheering here for you

No matter what the outcome
No matter which team scores
There'll be two winners on the field of proud ambassadors

Here's to you I say again
With sentiments so true
Lose or win, through thick or thin, we will follow you

Oh what a town for football
For here on Merseyside
We see the winner is our town, for humour sport and pride

Our all to you the Red and Blue
And when you come back home
There'll be a welcome and my lads . . . *You'll Never Walk Alone* . . .

***Norm Whittle***

**BRAMFORD**

It's got a well used village hall
Where the kids can have a ball,
(Also used for carpet bowls and keeping fit)
In the winter we have panto's
Where men get to wear the hose
It's all a hoot - and sometimes even a hit!

It's got tennis courts and bowling green
A football pitch for the young and keen
And a playgroup (if you're really rather tiny)
If you're bigger, it's got liquor -
The watering holes are quite superior
And we're fifteen miles away from the briney.

There's a river running through
(Gives the fishermen things to do)
In fact you often see quite a few canoes.
City trains occasionally belt through
Apart from that, only the odd moo
Disturbs a peaceful Sunday afternoon snooze.

Walking can be quite a pleasure
When you've got a spot of leisure
If you're feeling active, we've got a WI
We have no airs and graces
In fact, it's just one of those places
Where we residents, as a rule, see eye to eye.

Where is this awesome place
That is filled with charm and grace?
And doesn't give you time to be bored?
It's nearer than you suppose,
This mix of life and repose -
Allow me to introduce you to *Bramford!*

**Sue Rhodes**

## IRSTEAD STAITHE

At Irstead Staithe neat cropped grass
        leads to the water's edge
Where mallard sit anticipating
        visitors with crumbs of bread.
There is a seat and many hours
        are spent watching the craft
Drawing up, reversing back
        and mooring up at last.
People busy throwing ropes
        jump with agile grace
From boat to land and back again
        glad for a good night's base.
Willows dip the margins
        of the River Ant
Which opens out to Barton Braad
        home to many cormorant
And to the safety of the reeds
        coot and moorhen scurry
From the ripple rings of wash
        arising from the flurry

*Margaret Vernon*


## ROMAN CAMULODUNUM

Roman Cam-u-lo-du-num,
the capital on the Colne,
Colchester town, of high renown
you will not be overthrown.

The Roman Wall still standing
will keep aggressors at bay:
the Romans inside, alas have died,
but will never fade away.

The temple of your Caesar
was an imperial sight,
and Claudius saw just a temp'rary flaw
what Bou-dic-ca set alight.

Roman civilisation
brought your dignity home:
the Oystermen's bed, the fishermen said,
had all the pearls of Ancient Rome.

The Norman's tried their conquest,
the Cavaliers had their siege
but none of that kind could have undermined
Roman Colchester's prestige.

*Brian A Cooke*


## THE HOSPICE AT COLCHESTER

T his house of hope and kindliness,
H aven of love and cheerfulness,
E difice designed for those
S eeking quiet and repose;
T ranquillity here surrounds,
H appiness within abounds,
E ase from trouble and from cares,
L ightening the load one bears;
E nriching all with spiritual gain,
N umbing so much hurt and pain,
A rming all with new found zest
H ere within this house of rest,
O ozing virtues we hold dear
S weeping aside despair and fear;
P eace and quietude attends
I nside these portals and so lends
C omfort for all who with grace
E mbrace *the beauty* of this place . . .

*Ken Moore*

## MY STREET

The street where I live is not very wide
Lots of cars are parked on either side,
There's a little corner shop
That's open all day right up to ten o'clock,
I've lived in my house for nearly six years now
and I'm really happy here
It's not too far from the centre of town
everything from buses to trains are all so near
Everyone is so kind and friendly they wave or
stop and say hello
Even if they are rushing off to work they still
find time to have a chat before they go.
Nice to have neighbours who you can turn to
if you need them any time
Cards through doors at Christmas and they call
round to have a glass of wine,
Near the corner where I live there are lots
of School of Motoring everyone is trying to
learn to drive. Sometimes they come up on the path,
peeping behind the curtains looking at all
the mistakes they make I try and not to laugh.
I've lived in a lot of places and had a lot of
houses but this is the best I've known
When I've been out for the day or been away
it's nice to come back home

*Linda Roberts*

## WHY ESSEX?

Why choose Essex?
Well, I know why,
Variety.
From county city
To country village
Rolling farmland
Seaside funfair.
To sailing town
Or fishing village
All to be found
In proud Essex
Now, make a choice
Too difficult?
No, not for me.
Give me the tide
Out of Bradwell,
Into the open;
The Blackwater.
Wind now in sails
Reaching with joy.
Look and take in
Power Station,
Dark and brooding.
See St Peter's
And up river
Osea and on
Maldon in view.
Ever changing
Why choose Essex?

*Sonia J Lister*

## NORWICH CITY

Wander the streets of the city
        as generations before,
Absorb the historical atmosphere
        - and more.
                Walk through.

Climb to the castle,
        high on the mound,
Wander the battlements
        - cells underground.
                Walk through.

See above - the cathedral
        spire,
Pause awhile - hear the
        heavenly choir.
                Walk through.

Visit quaint buildings,
        courtyards - until
Before you see -
        cobbled Elm Hill.
                Walk through.

People come from near
        and afar
The gates to the city
        are always ajar.
                Walk through.

*D M Stone*

## THE MESSAGE OF THE BELLS

The bells ring out for joy
Ding dong! Ding dong! Ding dong!
O come with thankful hearts
And join the happy throng
In praise to Christ the King
The bells do gladly ring.

The bells ring out for peace
On this peninsula,
The peace of God to reign
In hearts both near and far.
Lord from our sins release
And let us know Your peace.

The bells ring out for hope,
That in the darkest days
Our Lord is there to guide
And order all our ways.
List to the message clear
And cast away all fear.

The bells ring out for love
This joyful Christmas-tide,
Love that came among us
Stay with us and abide.
God's great Love all excels
In the message of the bells.

*Maureen Crampin*

## THE KNIGHTS OF ESSEX '95

We owe so much to Essex
Look around you and you'll see
How much this precious piece of land
Provides for you and me.

It used to be horse and carriage
Which kept us all alive
But now lorries traverse the highways
By the Knights of Essex '95.

Trains and modern motorcars
Have changed the rural scene
And motorways and tunnels
Have fulfilled architects' dreams.

Now Essex man and woman;
Friends, relations, one and all
Can look around and travel
Beyond the suburban sprawl.

From London to the Channel
And sweeping down to the Thames
There are vistas in abundance
With a heritage of gems.

Now Essex is adjusting
To the hi-tech age
Still listening with nostalgia
To the country sage.

Year 2000 is dawning
And we must not lament
On all the joys of *has been*
And the happy times we spent.

**Barbara Fosh**

## NORWICH AND ITS NICHE IN THE UNIVERSE

There's reasons why the Castle glows at night
To burn from life, that shatters, that frights
On a belittled hill, for an ancient battle and modern retreat
A continuum of neglect scream the treadmill heels of a thousand feet

There's peace in swept rows of stalls so striped with sheets
In sun and moon tranquillity keeps, with one less voice to hurd everyday
Quiet wares withdraw from view, never fruitful, always blue
Enticement proves a life that is hard, though history grew

There's longing through ushered crowds of anxious meat, defeat
With eyes that strain to rise, to others chic and considerably meek
Standing at the human monkey who performs on cue *for you, for you*
An excuse to stop is an excuse to watch, a jester with a sensical
                                          invitation to flop

There's rhyme around a churchyard, while honest hearts hide
A dance and a jovial slip and a slide, bury with swigs of vile
A thundering friend offers money and time, evangelical decline
Rotary squawking, walking over paths of heads laden with grass for beds

There's old innocents huddled near a virtual spot, that progress
                                        somehow had to blot
Watching colourful acts of grime and insanity, all players
Missing manners and tea-rooms and opportunity knocks, they'd just forgot
Wishing summer to brighten new minds and other such rot

There's a wise old sky, high and ashamed, above the whole sorry lot
It has only to remain, to be King, to be God
There's a lesson to be learned by us mute volunteers
It's not about stepping up, but snuggling with our peers
All else, confusion and tears.

*Dale Craske*

## MARSH MILL

Motionless, silent, ghostly you stand,
A sad, poignant monument to ages past;
Your broken sails and neglected body a stark reminder
Of man's indifference to your once proud history.
Obstinately you pose defying the elements to do their worst,
A challenge which they accept with relish,
Unmercifully pounding your battered and decaying skin.
Your heart alas, beats no more, deprived of life sustaining grease
Which fed your unfailing mechanical core.
What secrets you hold dear friend in your disembodied heart,
What tales you could tell if only you could speak?
Faithful, geriatric guardian of marshland,
No more will you creak in the playful wind
But thankfully bathe in sunlight,
Gently repose in starlight,
A haunting, ghostly artefact under a radiant smiling moon.

*Malcolm F Andrews*


## KENT

Oh, to live in a garden
So vast you can't see the fence
With Spring orchards laid out in patchwork
The profusion of blossom so dense.

Oh, to live in a garden
Painstakingly planned through the years
Not tended with love by a family
But farmers through blood, sweat and tears.

Oh, to live in a garden
Where the summers are warm but not hot
And the evenings of Autumn are chilly
Drawn in by a curtain of hops.

Oh, to live in a garden
When the Winter snows are spent
For there in the mist of the morning
Lies the Garden of England, Kent.

**Lynda M Bourne**




### THE WINDS OF TIME

The Southeast Coast views distant sales
As a depth of mystery unveils
Seaward winds and landward gales
Fishermen with ancient tales
'Bout secret coves and secret bays
And smugglers in the olden days
Fighting through the sprawling waves
To the shelter of their dampened caves.

Endless streams of rock formation.
Secure within their destination
As though unchanged since lifes creation.
So still as if in meditation.
They watch with eyes the seabirds fly
Sweeping low and gliding high
In unknown realms of changing sky
As fading light shows dusk is nigh.

A lasting peace in a hectic world.

**D Cain**

## SILENCE AT THE MILL

Inside the noisy mill
Where racing belts
Flew over whining pulleys,
Driving machines
Of spinning bobbins
And flying shuttles.
Mill hands like ants
Scuttled about their work
From morn till eve,
Their lives controlled
By the mighty steam engine.

Majestic she stood
Her paint work gleaming
Dials and gauges glistening.
Her mighty fly wheel throbbing out
The tempo of industry.
Her eunuch, the engine tenter
Oiled and greased her every part,
Fed her insatiable appetite for coal
Hewn from deep mines,
And from her chimney stack
Billowed acrid smoke.

The chimney stack has long been felled
The mine shafts capped.
The mighty engine
Stands listless in a museum.
The engine tenter sleeps never to awake.
The mill is now a ghostly warehouse,
And the only sound of motion
Is the shuffle of a dole queue.

*David A Garside*

# INFORMATION

We hope you have enjoyed reading this book - and that you will continue to enjoy it in the coming years.

If you like reading and writing poetry drop us a line, or give us a call, and we'll send you a free information pack.

Write to

>Arrival Press Information
>1-2 Wainman Road
>Woodston
>Peterborough
>PE2 7BU.